The Human Side
of Leadership

The Human Side of Leadership

Navigating Emotions at Work

Rick Ginsberg and
Timothy Gray Davies

Westport, Connecticut
London

Library of Congress Cataloging-in-Publication Data

Ginsberg, Rick, 1952–
The human side of leadership : navigating emotions at work / Rick Ginsberg and Timothy Gray Davies.
    p. cm.
    Includes bibliographical references and index.
    ISBN-13: 978–0–275–99132–6 (alk. paper)
    1. Leadership—Psychological aspects.   2. Emotional intelligence.
3. Management—Psychological aspects.   I. Davies, Timothy Gray, 1942–   II. Title.
  HD57.7.G557   2007
  658.4′092—dc22   2007016224

British Library Cataloguing in Publication Data is available.

Library of Congress Catalog Card Number: 2007016224
ISBN-13: 978–0–275–99132–6

First published in 2007

Praeger Publishers, 88 Post Road West, Westport, CT 06881
An imprint of Greenwood Publishing Group, Inc.
www.praeger.com

Printed in the United States of America

The paper used in this book complies with the
Permanent Paper Standard issued by the National
Information Standards Organization (Z39.48–1984).

10 9 8 7 6 5 4 3 2 1

Rick Ginsberg: To Lauri, Matt, Alex, and Noah, for helping me to navigate through the emotions of work and life with the love and joy that only a family can provide.

Tim Davies: To my students and colleagues who have shared their emotions and their emotional experiences, and by doing so have made me a better person to become a better leader. God bless us, every one.

Contents

Preface

The work that underlies this book began with a simple friendship. We both had served in leadership roles over the course of our careers—in business, in community colleges, and in small and large universities. One of us only recently had left the lofty position of college president to become a faculty member, while the other had left the faculty ranks to lead an academic unit. We both were engaged in teaching leadership—one for nearly twenty years, the other in starting a new venture that involved developing an entire program for aspiring college presidents. Given our recent pasts and new challenges we developed a mutual respect and reciprocal relationship where we shared and addressed concerns with which each recently had been dealing.

Over the years our relationship evolved and our friendship endured. We learned from one another and grew together. We discovered a mutual interest in understanding how leaders deal with the emotional hardships. We shared many stories, laughs, and realized that our conversations treaded on areas that leadership scholarship had not addressed. We've each dealt with personal illnesses that may have been brought on by the nature of our leadership work. While we don't know, for example, if being a leader causes heart disease, the stress associated with the job can't help. Like many leaders, we have wives and kids who bring their own joys and fears and tribulations to the mix. That has affected our personal makeup as well, for all that we experience in our lives somehow combines to create who we are. But being a leader adds a certain level of responsibility that few others experience. People look to you for support, guidance, help, and answers. The old adage "the buck stops here" implies a heavy weight for the person carrying that buck! Being in charge carries a level of responsibility that others in the workplace don't experience, just as being a parent carries more responsibility than being a kid—it's just part of what is expected.

We shared how our leadership positions impacted our health, our marriages, and our friendships over our combined sixty years as leaders. Ultimately, a very simple research question kept coming up. How do leaders deal with the difficult emotional issues they confront? We found little in the books and journal articles we read that provided many clues. So we started our own research, and quickly found that others who were or had been leaders had similar questions as those we were discussing and trying to understand.

A poignant example came a few years ago when we were collecting stories for our original study related to the emotional impact that different kinds of decisions have on leaders. An organization composed of university leaders from all over the country invited us to their national meeting to talk about what we were learning. We had been involved with the group over the course of several years and readily agreed to meet with them as a means of validating or countering what we were learning. We attended their Chicago meeting, and on a cold windy winter afternoon we had the first chance to find out if what we were studying had any traction beyond the conversations we had been having among ourselves for nearly a decade. We agreed to this with the understanding that we would have about forty-five minutes to an hour on the agenda to talk about our research and answer any questions that might be raised. We also thought that our making such a presentation might convince a large number of those present to share their experiences with us. It was a win-win situation from our perspective, but frankly, we had no idea what the reaction would be to our work. Given that we weren't charging a fee, we figured that even if things didn't go well, the audience would feel satisfied that they had gotten exactly what they had paid for.

When the agenda arrived a few weeks before the meeting, we were dismayed to find that we were scheduled last on the one full day of the conference. In fact our presentation was set at 4:00 p.m. just before the 5:00 p.m. reception, which boasted free cocktails and substantial hors d'oeuvres. Anyone who has ever attended a conference knows that such an agenda placement is tantamount to talking to the kids during nap time at the local preschool. Attendees would be exhausted after a full day of meetings and sessions that had started at eight that morning. Many would probably leave to relax or freshen up before the heavy drinking began. Those who remained likely would be cordial and polite but not terribly engaged, as our talk would give them about sixty minutes to take the kind of eyes-wide-open catnaps that pervade such conferences. We figured we could prepare an interesting but brief presentation on our material with the intention of getting done a few minutes early. Surely nobody would be interested enough to waste time on questions, so we prepared about fifteen to twenty minutes of slides and conversation.

The actual meetings and sessions that preceded our talk were even more tiring than we had expected. People in the audience were visibly exhausted. We had planned a few jokes and humorous episodes gleaned from our data, so we started with those and went through the material as quickly as possible. After nearly twenty minutes, we finished and paused to get a sense of the audience's reaction to our work. The plan was to close by thanking them for their attendance and attention. Noting the heavy eyelids and occasional chin that was dropping to the table tops, we were pretty confident that we would be on our way very quickly after making the obligatory last comment:—"Are there any questions?" We were pleased that there had been no obvious snoring during our talk, and everyone had been ostensibly interested and very cordial. After a lull of nearly thirty seconds, we thanked everyone for being there and joked about getting through early enough so they could start the fun part of the evening.

But as we started picking up our note cards to leave, an elderly fellow sitting just in front of the podium raised his hand and asked about how our research related to that of a well-known scholar writing about leadership. What a surprise, we thought, that anyone had actually paid attention! We figured that he was just being polite and felt bad for us, sensing that everyone else was ready to jump out of their seats and head to the reception. After answering his question, we were shocked to see another hand shoot up, then another, and several others after that. This went on for nearly ninety minutes. We actually cut into the time for the hors d'oeuvres!

What we learned was that we had tapped into something that had been bottled up inside these leaders for years. Person after person lamented that nobody talked about the emotions with which she had to deal. They highlighted how lonely it was being the boss, how much more difficult this aspect of the job was than anything anticipated. Frankly, we could have stayed there all night answering questions and discussing the issues we raised had we not decided to put an end to the session. We left incredibly gratified, realizing that our work was treading on something that nobody ever talked about. It obviously wasn't the conversation that the leadership gurus ever harped on, but it was clear that the emotions that leaders grapple with during the course of their work is something that deserves greater attention.

The obvious lack of attention to the dark side of dealing with emotions in leadership is something that amazes us as we learn more and more about the topic. In business, hospital administration, public school leadership, the military, and other fields, the training programs that are available simply ignore the issue. We could find no state standards, for example, that guide the certification of principals and superintendents, which require any preparation on dealing with the emotions of being a leader. We found no MBA programs that have this as an integral part of what they present. No courses, no emphasis, nothing. Emotions, if even mentioned at all, are seen as something that leaders should use as a way to motivate their workers. Jump up, scream, get excited, and implore the troops to seek greater heights, but never grapple with how the emotions that your decisions evoke may impact your life and ability to lead.

It's worse in academia. In our world, where we provide credentials for leaders entering an array of professions, there is no preparation required for those we place in positions of leadership. Society's main credentialing institution, the university, has no credential requirements for its department chairs, deans, vice presidents, provosts, chancellors, and presidents, other than the advanced degree required to earn a teaching position in their academic discipline. But when it comes to leadership positions in the academic world, it's experience that counts. Seems hypocritical to us, but in terms of preparation for dealing with emotions, we can say with absolute certainty that there is no training or preparation offered for leaders in the academy.

So we undertook our research and wrote this book with confidence that we are heading where few have gone before. Like the *Enterprise* in Star Trek, we are visiting new places for researchers to explore and understand. The emerging research on the significance of emotions in the workplace makes us believe that the areas we touch upon will continue to grow in importance for future generations of scholars to study. For if we have learned anything during the course of our research and preparation of this book, it is this: Being successful as a leader involves a great deal of emotional navigating. Leaders must deal with their own emotional reactions as well as those of the people they lead. It makes no difference if the organization is hierarchical or horizontal with decentralized decision making. Dealing with emotions is top down, bottom up, and side to side as workers certainly affect leaders as much as leaders affect them. Our hope is that by reading this short book, leaders, and those considering leadership positions, will embrace the importance of dealing with the emotions that will affect them on the job. It will require some forethought and introspection, but the planning that is necessary has the potential for enormous payoffs. It can make your stay as a leader far more satisfying and successful, and keep you happier and healthier than many of your peers.

Any undertaking such as this requires the help of a great many people. We first want to thank Dr. Jerry Gilley, who pushed us to take our research to book length and even started the negotiations for us with Praeger Publishers. Dr. Karen Multon and Dr. Jim Lichtenberg at the University of Kansas provided valuable insights and ideas that impacted the way the work unfolded. Adrian Henderson Douglas and Bruce Douglas at Colorado State University provided important assistance with library work that proved significant for us in grasping the full extent of the research available on emotions and emotional intelligence. Sophia Woodard of North Carolina A&T University helped us early on with several interviews with leaders from around the country.

To those who participated in our research, through providing stories, allowing formal interviews and less formal conversations, your willingness to share your perspectives and experiences have contributed in untold ways to the success of our research. We learned more from your lives and experiences than we ever anticipated, and hope that the publication of this book provides an apt substantiation for the many insights about emotions and leadership that you provided. We can't thank you enough.

As we write this, we're both in significant leadership positions and continue to rely upon one another to plow through the emotional issues that emerge in our very separate worlds. We hope that the things we've learned over the past ten years provide you with some insights to help guide you through the emotional waters that all leaders deal with.

Rick Ginsberg, Ph.D., University of Kansas
Timothy Gray Davies, Ph.D., Colorado State University

CHAPTER 1

"The Emotional Maze of Leadership"

I can't believe it. Another Sunday night and I can't fall asleep. I must have been tossing and turning for five hours. How many stupid sheep do I have to count! Let's see, if I fall asleep now I can get in three hours before rushing to my first meeting. Darn, I hate nights like this. It's just that horrible meeting I had with the staff last week. Everyone left so angry at me. What did they expect me to do? I figured that we could save a few jobs by cutting salaries equally across the board, and those idiots came down on me like I was the enemy. Geez, I should have gone along with the boss' suggestion and just selectively fired people . . . then they would really have gone ballistic. No, I went out of my way to protect everyone. They have no clue what I did for them. But I can't fire them. They're the best group I ever worked with . . . my friends. Sure, a few need a swift kick in the pants every once in a while, but that is to be expected. They're a great team. Oh, what am I going to do? I've got to get some sleep.

Sound familiar? Those sleepless nights talking to yourself and perseverating about something at work? No matter what you do you just can't let go, relax, and fall asleep. And yet you know that what you did what was right; it was in everyone's best interest. But that isn't always the case. There are times when you are equally flustered by not knowing what to do, or now and then you find yourself feeling guilty about something you did or a hasty decision you made. Harvard Business ethics professor Joseph Badaracco, Jr., describes the difficulty leaders incur when facing decisions in right versus right situations[1]—a dilemma experienced when there are two right ways to resolve a difficult situation. Each carries its own ethical and moral implications, yet a choice must be made. In this sleepless-night scenario, you really were trying to look out for everyone. The great UCLA basketball coach John Wooden once remarked that the "softest pillow is a clear conscience." Yet here you are on another Sunday night, tossing and turning and unable to get to sleep. What's up?

Business and professional leaders told us story after story that identified emotionally laden situations in which decisions took their toll on everyone involved. One memorable story involved Betty, a sixty-five year-old employee of a manufacturer who ran the billing and shipping department. Known as "the invoice queen," she was, through sheer hard work and longevity, promoted to supervisor. She was a stoic character who was very conservative and wore what was characterized as a 1950s style "beehive" hairdo. She had a very prim and proper approach to the people with whom she worked. Everyone agreed that she was a nice person set in her ways and hadn't changed the way she did her job for thirty-five years. The computer was her enemy, an evil innovation reducing her personal control over the organization. She saw no benefits to the newer computerized systems, and those machines were something "for the younger ones" who didn't take the time to learn to handle their responsibilities in a "proper way."

Still, everyone admired her. She was like the business's mother hen: dependable, constant, and willing to show any employee, especially the new hires, the company's way to conduct business. She hadn't missed a day of work since she her last child was born some thirty years ago. Her coworkers often lamented, "What would we do without Betty?" Many would have been shocked to learn that they soon would find out.

Management despised her! They wanted her gone. She was a roadblock to integrating their newer ideas and running the department more efficiently. But not Jay, an entry-level manager who completed a three-month management training period. Fresh out of college he was amused that little Betty engendered such fear among management team members. He liked her. He got a kick out of this "retro figure" in a company that constantly talked of cutting-edge technology and being leaders in their field. Besides, Betty had been very nice to him since he joined the company.

Much to his dismay, Jay's vice-president told him to fire Betty. He was told she would thank him for freeing her up, allowing her to spend more time with her husband and grandchildren. She would retire with a healthy pension. "You'll be doing her a favor by letting her go. Just tell her that her services are no longer needed." It was little help in consoling his anxiety.

Poor Jay struggled for days, pondering how he would tell Betty she was fired. He slept little and his stomach was constantly upset, so he kept postponing firing Betty. But then his boss confronted him. He asked when her last day would be. Finally, the fateful encounter occurred. Jay started to cry before he could say anything to Betty. She just hugged him and told him that everything would be okay.

Emotions are powerful forces and basic to mankind: anger, fear, happiness, disgust, sadness, surprise, and contempt.[2] Remember when you first fell in love? You were on top of the world! Nothing could wake you from your heavenly dream. Dean Martin's old song expressed the emotion well: *When you walk in a dream and know you're not dreamin', signoré, s'excusé me, but you see, back in old Napoli, that's amoré.* Love surely is grand . . . if only all emotions had you floating back in old Napoli. Being happy is a tonic for so many ills. But psychologists have documented that other emotions can doggedly bring you down as well. Fear, for example, can grip your soul and cause severe stress and anxiety. Scholars argue that fear has a "toxic effect."[3] Likewise, anger, whether a divorce or a job-related situation, becomes a ball and chain around your leg, slowing you down, holding you back, making you less productive. Guilt, jealousy, and other negative emotions can impact your ability to think clearly. Sometimes these emotions are so pronounced that you just can't seem to let go and the matter is hard to forget. Reactions to emotional states cause paralysis, denial, avoidance, vacillation, and errant judgment. Emotions can overwhelm even the strongest individual, and everyone has experienced the incredible power they wield. Oxford University Psychology Professor Edmund Rolls tells us:

> The puzzle is not that the emotion is so intense, but also that even with our rational, reasoning capacities, humans still find themselves in these situations, and may find it difficult to produce reasonable and effective decisions and behavior for resolving the situation.[4]

But now you *are* the boss. You have significant responsibilities and are expected to lead people and produce specific outcomes. Much like you felt about your parents when you were young, you have an overriding sense that you should be omnipotent. You're the one everyone looks to for guidance, direction, and support; you're supposed to behave in a certain way. Likewise, you hear information that is shared with no one else. You know more about your employees than you ever cared to learn. You're aware of pending personnel cuts, you are sworn to secrecy, and you cannot share the specifics. You have to keep it all to yourself.

Your workers, colleagues, and staff rely on your strength to lead the organization. It is a tremendous responsibility, and many people expect their leaders to exhibit a certain demeanor as they discharge their responsibilities.

Years ago, the media ridiculed presidential candidate Edmund Muskie when he cried after having heard negative comments concerning his wife. Sports commentators, writers, and fans mocked former Kansas City Chiefs football coach Dick Vermeil because he would become overly emotional—to the point of tears—when defending his team. As the Tom Hanks' character lamented to his female ballplayers in the popular movie, *A League of Their Own*, "There's no crying in baseball!" Nor do we expect any crying in the boss's office. The face, the image, the expectations are the burden placed on those we ask to lead. Fair or unfair, like it or not, the positional leader sets the organization's tone, and our culture holds certain expectations for the leader's behavior.

Maddock and Fulton, in their book, *Motivation, Emotions, and Leadership*, provide a simple characterization of this dilemma for leaders:

> The leader is just another individual. . . . They put their pants on just like the rest of us do. They have both good and bad traits. From time to time, when things are going badly, their old character traits slip through and they become irritable, angry, irrational and capricious. They behave in immature ways. They exhibit traits that amaze us and we say, "I always thought of him/her as a leader! What's going on?" They disappoint us.[5]

So the reality is you are human. You're a parent, a friend, a spouse, a colleague, a Democrat, a Republican, a person with feelings, ideas, values, and morals just like everyone else. And while you know that you are fully qualified and prepared for this position, nobody warned you about the emotional side of being in charge. There is no preparing for finding emotional serenity when you assume leadership; there is no graduate degree or certificate to earn, no pill to take to make the rough feelings go away. You're on your own. You will face emotionally laden decisions that will haunt you for days and weeks at a time. It is inevitable. There will come a day when you and an employee are eyeball to eyeball, and you have to let him go, turn down her promotion or raise, perhaps share a bad evaluation, or negatively critique an idea he has suggested. It is never easy.

One leader described the time a close friend, a colleague for years, was in his office to discuss his yearly merit evaluation. His friend had performed poorly that year, so he tried to soften the blow labeling the evaluation "about average." His friend screamed, "I have never worked so hard in my life to be rated as average." He was taken aback. The outburst hurt him emotionally especially since he had worried about this meeting and how to soften the blow for several weeks. You will experience these kinds of emotional reactions to many of your decisions. Another leader told us that his wife was worried that the job was taking an unbearable toll on his health and that it might be time to quit. "No," he said, "it's when you stop having these emotional feelings that it is time to get out of the business."

All leaders experience this emotional pain. Nobody is immune, not even the great ones. Lee Iacocca describes the emotional drawbacks he experienced turning around Chrysler Corporation. Despite what he called the "equality of sacrifice," having everyone share in making adjustments for the company to move ahead, there was emotional sacrifice as well. While lauding the family atmosphere that evolved to allow the fix to take hold, there was the "dark side":

> But our struggle also had its dark side. To cut expenses, we had to fire a lot of people. It was like a war: we won, but my son didn't come back. There was a lot of agony. People were getting destroyed, taking their kids out of college, drinking, getting divorced. Overall we preserved the company, but only at an enormous personal expense for a great many human beings.[6]

How you react to your personal emotions will have profound consequences for your organization. Emotions affect your collegial relationships and organizational decisions. Regarding these relationships, researchers have shown that your expressions and the verbal images you employ as you converse with others affect your communication by emphasizing or amplifying messages. Even your unconscious facial expressions or emotions convey messages that explain your standing with others in your organization. Your emotional state and how you express it affects your company, business, or institution. Moreover, if you are able to evoke the proper emotions, the result may be altering behavior in followers.[7] Emotions may impact what you decide. Research on female leaders' decision making has demonstrated that some emotions produce more autocratic decisions when there were threats to stereotypes.[8] Sam Intrator's description of how new teachers affect their students captures quite well the issue of a leader's potential impact on coworkers in an organizational setting:

> When beginning teachers stand before students, they are not merely enacting a curriculum or behaving according to prescribed protocols but also are individuals with an emotional makeup and way of being that irretrievably shape how others will experience them. My beginning teachers quickly learn that students will study their vulnerabilities, moods, emotional triggers with the attention to detail of a jeweler drilling pearls.[9]

You planned and prepared for your leadership move for a long time. You expected the added work and pressure. You anticipated the increased prestige, the additional compensation, and the thought that you would make a real difference. But most important, you knew in your heart that you had the ability to do the job well. Thus, you accepted this new role. You thought, "all those idiots I have worked for over the years. I can do this!" But now it's Sunday night and you can't get to sleep ... again. You're emotionally spent and wondering if the positives outweigh the negative feelings you are experiencing. Why didn't anyone warn you about this emotional side of being a leader? How do others cope with all this?

Experts who analyze ethical decision making have emphasized that using a "sleep-test" is no guarantee your leadership decision was right or wrong. Indeed, having trouble sleeping may be an indication that you are on the right path. Joseph Badaracco reminded us that many doctors spent days committing unthinkable atrocities during the Holocaust, then sat down to pleasant family dinners. On the other hand, he explained:

> ... responsible people sometimes lie awake at night *precisely because they have done the right thing* [authors' emphasis]. They understand that their decisions have real consequences, that success is not guaranteed, and that they will be held accountable for their decisions. They also understand that acting honorably and decently can, in some circumstances, complicate or damage a person's career. In short, if people like Hitler sometimes sleep well and if people like Mother Teresa sometimes sleep badly, we can place little faith in simple sleep-test ethics.[10]

But even knowing your sleeplessness may be for all the right reasons doesn't diminish the fact that you emotionally are drained.

One problem you will face in dealing with the emotional fallout of your decisions is that it is impossible to predict what response they will elicit. Too often, there is little rationale in the responses to your decisions. To underscore this simple proposition we share an exercise we use with employee groups with whom we work. Though we don't know for certain who first developed this exercise, we call it "The Square Game" (see Figure 1.1). We ask audience members to write down how many squares they see in the table. No talking is permitted. Then we go around the room and ask participants how many squares they counted. The variation of responses will surprise you as much as it always surprises us.

For many, it is a simple mathematical solution solved by multiplying four squares by four squares to arrive at sixteen. We have heard many times in

Figure 1.1
The Square Game

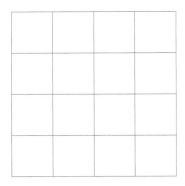

many settings that sixteen has to be the right answer! Others, however, add the large square that houses all the other squares and their answer is seventeen. Some get creative and count the four two-by-two squares in each corner and come up with twenty-one as their response. But then, of course, there are other two-by-two squares and three-by-three squares, so the answers can pile up. One time an audience participant told us that he knew this was a trick question and remembered hearing somewhere that the "right answer" was 236! We just shook our heads and didn't ask for the mathematical calculation.

The point, of course, is that there isn't a "right" answer. Even with this most simple exercise using an inanimate one-dimensional table, the disagreement on the response that the question engenders is remarkable. Now add the human psyche, feelings, values, and emotions and just consider what the possible range of responses to a decision you make might provoke. Our philosophically relativist friends have a point here when they tell us that each person's reality is created by that person and the idea of an objective "truth" doesn't fit when dealing with human beings and their cornucopia of emotions.

To this point, we have been addressing you as though you were the leader in charge. Perhaps not in charge of your entire company, but we have addressed you as though you were a positional leader with an official title and responsible for a section or department within the organization. Just as there are numerous "correct" answers to the Square Game, there are other organizational leaders besides the titled positional leaders who also are affected by the emotional side of leadership. So, looking back at our positional leader tossing and turning in his bed, it is not hard to visualize that he is not the only person going sleepless, and his is not the only "Truth" being examined. Positional leaders in hierarchical organizations often feel they are the only ones who care about the employees and the employees' families. They feel that they have the right answers, and the most "just" way to resolve potentially dangerous situations, and they alone shoulder the ultimate safety of everyone in their organization. But the organization is a kaleidoscope, and when a different employee twists the kaleidoscope's ring a new mosaic is created. A mosaic that is different but perhaps just as accurate. To think that only positional leaders care for others is not only egotistical but also dangerous. For right across town from our sleepless positional leader is the informal employee leader. The one to whom many rank and file look for reassurance and trusted guidance. Every department has at least one. In fact even positional leaders search them out to "try" new ideas and possible solutions. Unfortunately, our informal leader also is lying awake this Sunday evening.

Damn him! Off he goes again on his own without consulting with us at all. I know deep down he has our interest at heart. I know the others don't always believe that and this new decision won't help me convince them either. Why can't he come talk to us? Why can't he help us understand the problems and challenges the company is facing? We are all in this together! When all is going well, he comes around and talks and shares. But when there is a problem, he hides out and then the next we know a decision is made "in our best interests" without our best thinking being added to the mix. He thinks he rides in on his white horse and saves us. I'd like to shoot his white horse. Then maybe he would help us understand the problem and not just the decision. I still can't sleep. Maybe if I email him I will feel better.

Our informal leader sees the Square Game in a different context. How do our organizations neglect the informal leaders and rely only on the positional leaders? No wonder why there are such radically different perceptions of what the real problems and challenges are when we only view them through one set of lenses. Currently, there is talk among organizational leaders about inclusiveness and participatory decision making and the talk flows smoothly and is embraced by all. Until, that is, a situation arises that positional leadership determined information can flow only one way. In the instant that decision becomes reality, the informal leaders and their followers are left to their own devices. It is at this point that the emotional side of leadership becomes the challenge.

So how best to navigate through this emotional maze and the potential effects that they may have on you and your work as a leader? This book addresses emotional leadership, something missing in our leadership and training programs. One might think that since leadership is so people-oriented that there would be a focus on the inevitable emotional entanglements that pervade human interactions. But emotions have been treated as something to avoid even though they are being recognized as potentially useful forces for motivating employees and ourselves to greater productivity. But what about you? Whether you are a positional leader or an informal leader within your organization, you realize that tapping people's emotional energy can help boost their performance, excitement, and joy for their work. However, it is also true that all emotions aren't positive. And just as you try to evoke effective types of emotions in working with your employees and coworkers, you are affected by reactions to you and your decisions. What are the types of decisions that cause leaders to hesitate, to perseverate, and to struggle with making a response or dealing with its effectiveness? How do you move on?

We have spent considerable time thinking about and studying this issue. The literature examining human emotions, motivation, and leadership has expanded geometrically in the past two decades. When this literature, representing a wide array of academic disciplines is put together, we end up with testaments to the power of emotions in promoting workplace productivity. But leadership studies have ignored this emotional side of being a leader and how these emotions can take over your life and affect your performance.

Research that speaks to the power that emotions play in our lives is the work on emotional intelligence popularized by Dan Goleman and his colleagues.[11] It focuses on the power that emotional competence can have. According to Salovey and Mayer, emotional intelligence is a form of social intelligence "that involves the ability to monitor one's own and others' emotions, to discriminate among them, and to use the information to guide one's thinking and actions."[12] People high in emotional intelligence are more successful in their lives and work; to many its power is seen as more important than general intelligence. Tests for gauging emotional intelligence have been developed, even forms particularly geared toward the leader's emotional intelligence. Mayer and Salovey underscore the potential effects of emotional intelligence this way:

Different types of people will be more or less emotionally intelligent. Emotionally intelligent individuals may be more aware of their own feelings and those of others. They may be more open to positive and negative aspects of internal experience, better able to label them, and when appropriate, communicate them. Such awareness will often lead to the effective regulation of affect within themselves and others, and so contribute to well being.[13]

Clearly, the work on emotional intelligence is related to the issues that have perplexed leaders for years. Being emotionally competent is an ingredient in anyone's success. Leadership and organizational behavior studies that have touched upon emotions see them as a utilitarian tool to help meet the bottom line. Obviously, emotions can have an impact on people. But how various decisions that have emotional outcomes affect you and your leadership role remains unexplored. We've come to respect the fact that leaders carry a dual burden regarding emotions because they *both* induce and experience the fallout when decisions are rendered. We turned to leaders throughout various contexts to learn how they were affected by those highly emotional decisions. We talked with positional leaders and informal leaders in different organizations. Over and over again we learned that leaders bear an incredible responsibility for the impact their decisions have on their staff. We also learned that leaders experience personal emotional fallout. In this book we explore the emotional side of leadership. Our hope is to take you down a path that you inevitably will confront and ultimately help you think about ways to deal with the emotional interactions you will experience.

PLAN FOR THE BOOK

In this book we hope to share what already is known about issues like leadership, emotions, and emotional intelligence. Then, drawing from research we have conducted, set out a series of issues and themes related to the concern we have with how leaders are impacted by the emotions they face on the job. We'll close with some ideas on preparing leaders for the emotional circumstances they undoubtedly will be facing during the course of their tenure as boss. We'll also provide some insights about sources we have found particularly useful or interesting related to the issues addressed throughout the book.

In Chapter 2, "Framing the Issues: Emotions and Leadership," we examine research findings from a variety of fields to build a fuller understanding of the issues related to the leadership and the emotions they inevitably face when difficult decisions are rendered. Specifically, we'll review literature on leadership, emotions, intelligence, and emotional intelligence, and discuss various related matters like job stress and burnout and how our culture analyzes and defines the concept of success. The purpose is to provide an understanding of factors that have a research base that can help in understanding the job-related emotions that leaders confront.

Then, in the next several chapters, we begin to examine the data we've amassed from a variety of leaders from across the country on the emotional side of being in a leadership role. In Chapter 3, "The Eye of the Storm: The Agony of Decision Making," we present findings we derived from stories collected from leaders representing educational and business organizations on how their decisions affected them emotionally. A series of themes we synthesized are developed to explain the common issues. We follow in Chapter 4 with a focus on a special set of circumstances, what we call the "Extra Grace Required" colleague. Here we examine what can be done in dealing with a difficult employee, with special attention to being a leader when a friend causes some discomfort. We then turn to the whole issue of coping with the emotions that follow making a difficult decision. In Chapter 5, "Coping with Emotions on the Job," we pull a series of themes from our data that represent the kinds of coping mechanisms that the leaders we spoke with employed to deal with the emotional states they found themselves in.

In Chapter 6, "Planning for an Emotional Future," we set out a series of strategies, some we've derived from our work, others captured from the growing literature on emotions and emotional intelligence, to help you prepare yourself for the kinds of reactions you'll likely be dealing with as a leader. We offer a set of twelve lessons to help you build your emotional plan. Chapter 7, "Epilogue," provides some closure to our thinking by going back to several of the stories presented earlier in the book to show how their emotional work actually paid off. It provides an appropriate ending to our argument that leaders need to pay attention to and prepare for the emotional side of being in charge. We close with a story involving a situation we went through that displays how even the closest of friends in workplace interactions, even those ostensibly attuned to the human side of leadership, must plan for dealing with their emotions.

Last, at the end of the book, you'll find an annotated list of additional reading and resources for those who are interested.

A NOTE ON OUR DATA SOURCES

Throughout this book we will be drawing quotations and stories from leaders we interacted with through our formal research and in conversations we've held over the course of several years. The original research collected stories from leaders in education settings, including principals, superintendents, academic deans from four-year institutions of higher education, and presidents from community colleges.[14] In that study, we set out some very broad questions and asked the leaders to provide us with information about an experience they had in their leadership role that caused an emotional response on their part. We provided the leaders with guidelines as to how to construct their stories, e.g., the setting, the situation, what happened, how they responded, etc. Following that study, we have had purposeful conversations about the topic of dealing with emotions in the workplace with leaders representing a wide array of occupations. We call these purposeful conversations, because we held these discussions with individuals from various businesses in order to validate the findings we had identified in the formal research study. In all, we have collected stories or had conversations with several hundred leaders.

In reporting the quotations and stories in this book, we disguised the names of the leaders and the settings where they work. We also created a composite for some of the stories by drawing elements from similar conversations together. In all instances our purpose was to honor the anonymity and confidentiality of those whom we spoke with, while always staying true to the essence of the information they shared with us.

CHAPTER 2

Framing the Issues: Emotions and Leadership

What makes a leader special? Did you ever think about the makeup of po-litical icons or the bosses you admired and wondered what it was that made the great ones stand out? Franklin Roosevelt connected to the masses through his fireside chats. John Kennedy and his wife evoked images of a gilded past, the age of Camelot. They touched us, moved us, and somehow made us feel better. Daniel Goleman and his associates in their book about emotional intel-ligence and leadership provide an intriguing insight in trying to answer these questions:

> Great leaders move us. They ignite our passion and inspire the best in us. When we try to explain why they are so effective, we speak of strategy, vision, or powerful ideas. But the reality is much more primal. Great leadership works through the emotions.[1]

But just as the great ones may evoke strong emotions in the people they lead, leaders themselves are affected by the interactions with those they serve. Emotions can be a two-way street, and as is true with every aspect of life, there are frustrations and joys associated with any line of work. Emotions creep into the workplace for leaders, not just in the passion, anger, or other emotions that employees experience, but also within the leaders who must deal with the sometimes harsh reality of making difficult decisions. We're reminded of Janis, a well-recognized leader at a big state university. Her business mir-rored all service industries, being very people intensive. Key tasks for her in-clude: strengthening human-to-human contact, enhancing productivity, and promoting greater quality. Janis said she isn't able to measure effectiveness as objectively as some businesses can, because "there is no simple bottom-line." Her state-funded university is governed by Constitutional, legislative, and state regulatory guidelines. Yet, despite these differences, she struggled with the leadership complications that many share. She found it was nearly impossible to get people to change their ways.

Janis detailed her position's specific idiosyncrasies. College professors act like freelance agents who have extensive discipline expertise, and they won't consider alternative behavior. "It's like herding cats," she told us. "They look at me with a blank-stare when I suggest they consider different alternatives. Maybe it's no different in the private sector, I just don't know. But I do know that when I see faculty creating incredibly complex and inefficient programs, or holding to admissions and graduation policies that are not user-friendly, I find it virtually impossible to convince them to consider other ways of per-forming." It takes a toll on her.

> I stay awake at nights thinking about the stupidity of what they do, and no amount of my urging can make them look outside their comfort zone. The vast majority are tenured faculty, and I don't have needed leverage to get them to change. It drives me crazy! I get incredibly angry, but there is just no way for me to tell them to do something different, "or else!" I assume it's easier for leaders at Hewlett Packard or Microsoft. I also wonder how other deans get their faculty to change. I feel pathetic when I think about it. I just want to slam my door shut and scream at the top of my lungs, "What's wrong with me, why can't I make them understand?" Sometimes I believe that being a dean is the least powerful job on the planet. It makes me want to jump back to the classroom and laboratory, weave my little cocoon, and behave just like those faculty who infuriate me.

Perhaps Janis is being harder on herself than she deserves. Researchers have argued that getting people in educational organizations to change is akin to effecting a religious conversion.[2] But her experiences as a dean cap-ture the essence many leaders confront. Our culture is changing dramatically and leaders need to develop strategies to motivate or inspire their colleagues to change also. The demands are heavy.

Notice the technological advancement affecting our society. Our phones serve as cameras, minicomputers, daily scheduling calendars, text message systems, e-mail retrieval devices, and homing signals to track our children. The handy "Day at a Glance" calendar scheduling books we used to carry around are a prior century dinosaur. Fifteen years ago text messaging was not foreseen, the Internet was in its infancy, and the World Wide Web a wild-eyed prediction. Years ago Google was something that babies did. We couldn't exist without e-mail today though nobody had it when we started working a few decades ago. They were stuck using what today is called "snail-mail." Today's televisions are thin and flat and have screens of plasma. Isn't that something you used to donate with blood? Millionaires are hopping on rocket ships for sport. Music moved from simply being an audio experience on records, V-8s, and cassettes, to something on videos and CDs—and now into the current disk-free IPOD. Cars are keyless. Don't close your eyes for too long or you'll wake up and not understand how to turn on your lights (hint, just clap your hands).

The pace of technological change is dizzying, yet leaders must stay on top of such changes and integrate them into their organizations' culture. But technology isn't the only field where change has upended our world. Scientists have made discoveries that affect our health care and even our understanding of the human body and human nature. Santa Fe Institute researchers, for example, have changed thinking about science and developed research on complex adaptive systems. Drawing from studies on quantum physics, they have shown that our prior beliefs concerning the predictability and linearity of live systems is inaccurate.[3] Social science was built on the early Newtonian principles that dominated all science; the idea that the world is like a machine that behaves according to consistent behavioral rules. The complexity scientists have uncovered, however, that open systems operate less predictably than thought. This is what the great philosopher of science, Sir Karl Popper, captured when he suggested that, when thinking about the world, we move from seeing things like a clock to something more like a cloud.[4] To his thinking, the problem with notions like "survival of the fittest," is that "fittest" is only defined as having survived. Hard-and-fast, simple rules no longer apply. Similarly, human organization and human behavior theory development have new models suggesting that human beings and interactions among people don't follow the same rules that apply in test tubes. Indeed, if the world were so predictable, we would never lose money investing in the stock market, our children would learn everything, and all businesses would show a profit.

New thinking also has affected our understanding of emotions and leadership. In the next several pages we'll show how research has evolved in understanding interrelated issues like leadership, intelligence, emotions, and emotional intelligence. These changing conceptions help demonstrate why it is essential to appreciate the impact of emotions on leadership. We'll also highlight aspects of job stress and burnout, as well as conceptions of job-related success, because these, too, have an emotional impact on leaders as they lead.

WHAT WE KNOW ABOUT LEADERSHIP

> For thousands of years, people have known about the importance of effective leaders. Numerous leaders throughout history have written treatises on how to be effective as a leader, including individuals such as Alexander the Great, Marcus Aurelius, Lao Tsu, and St. Ignatius of Loyola.... Whether we read "how to" books by various experts, or biographies of successful leaders from industry, politics, or the military, it appears that many of us inherently know how important the skills and abilities of leadership are to our own lives.[5]

The earlier leadership mantra was that great leaders are born, not made. Early leadership theory research focused on successful leadership traits.[6] But if everyone seriously held that all there was to leadership was having the right genes, we doubt that so many leadership training and degree programs would exist in fields like business, healthcare, and education. No state has a law that requires businessmen and women to obtain an MBA to be in a leadership role, yet most leaders earn one anyway. Most fields require education or training and a highly prized credential to enter leadership.

Understanding leadership is complicated because different language is used in the research literature. One specific example to our current discussion revolves around the terms management and leadership. Do they mean the same thing? Require the same skill set? One leader told us a story about a former employee he knew would be a great manager, but he didn't have the "right stuff" to be an effective leader. The difference, as best as we could determine, was that this person had the ability to handle the sticky day-to-day issues for the business, but he didn't have the vision to lead the organization through the murky world of change. We all read about leaders who are depicted as charismatic, visionary, inspirational, and sometimes ruthless, creating the image that a leader is able to plow through difficult fields to move the company forward. This is the distinction some researchers and theorists describe as the difference between leadership and management.[7] Why these activities would be mutually exclusive was beyond the discussion we were having, so we didn't pursue that line of reasoning, but it captures a fundamental dilemma in the leadership scholarship.

Today, leadership is the more acceptable term, while manager or management is far less fashionable. Yet there is a long research history on managers and management at all levels of business and other organizations. From the very beginning, the Frederick Taylor rationalistic work required high degrees of control and dominated thinking on the subject.[8] In reaction, Henry Mintzberg moved management thinking beyond the "cerebral" or rational job components to what he called the "insightful" aspects of management.[9] However, two Dutch researchers shed light on a reality that confounds all the research. They explained, "although many books and papers have been devoted to the question of what it takes to be a good manager, little sound research has been performed in this area, and even less sound empirical research has specifically focused on top managers."[10]

Perhaps it is these "top managers" that some see as leaders, with those occupying the lower-level positions the mere managers. But in our study, it was clear that those in positions well below the level of CEO certainly felt that they were leaders performing their roles.

Our own perspective is that management refers to executing the daily functions necessary for an organization to persist, while leadership encompasses these managerial skills as well as the visionary and inspirational skills related to changing and improving the organization. We don't separate management and leadership, but instead view them as interrelated and complementary aspects necessary for an effective organization. They are significant, coexisting components. Good leaders are good managers, or they have the insight to surround themselves with individuals capable of doing the managerial tasks that leadership entails. Whatever your political leanings, one could argue that along with his obvious rhetorical gifts, it was Ronald Reagan's ability to surround himself with individuals who could attend to details he wasn't inclined to or capable of dealing with that helped make him such an effective leader.

What is interesting is that leadership literature has evolved apart from the management literature. Leadership theories have transcended cultures, generations, and theoretical beliefs. Typically, when leadership theory is taught, it is defined by the leaders' traits, qualities, and behaviors,[11] and the research has been grouped into three similar categories: traits, behaviors, and contingencies or situations.[12] First, trait research often espoused the "great man" or the charismatic leader. Early writers felt that capturing the great leaders' traits would help assess and identify these qualities.[13] More recently, researchers identified a plethora of attributes that leaders need to succeed including vision, core values, listening ability, and change strategies.[14]

Second, theoretical research emerged that focused on what leaders do—their behaviors—rather than the traits they possessed. The Ohio State University and the University of Michigan studies were the first behavioral studies from which instruments were developed to assess the individual leader's behavioral components.[15]

Third, situational and contingency leadership theories suggested that different leadership styles would be appropriate in differing contexts. These theorists examined the situations and developed instruments to measure the local context to help determine the most apropos leadership style. In essence, these theories brought together the other two theories, suggesting that analyzing the leader and the situation would identify the behaviors to be pursued.[16]

In more recent years, leadership theories and studies have continued to emerge that attempt to uncover relationships between leadership and organizational effectiveness. These newer theories purport to capture heretofore ignored issues such as: culture or cultural management, including the ability to understand the organizational culture and to modify it to assist with change;[17] leader and follower motivation studies;[18] and gender and spiritual aspects of leadership.[19] Manz and Sims have coined the phrase "Superleadership," challenging the single individual "spurring on workers" concept with the idea of someone helping others to lead themselves.[20] Others refer to this concept as "distributed leadership."[21] Margaret Wheatley has applied her new science notions derived from the research on complex adaptive systems to better understand how leadership should evolve given the way human systems actually operate.[22] Even Peter Senge, who introduced learning communities, has detailed how leadership for learning communities should differ from traditional leadership behavior notions.[23]

In industrial contexts, transactional leadership theory emerged, encompassing the leader-and-follower interchange or some service transaction for reward. Bass describes transactional leaders as those who explain what is required of workers in exchange for contingent rewards.[24] Transformational leadership theory evolved as more encompassing and realistic in the current context than the transactional theories. Rost describes transformational theory as characteristic of the postindustrial leadership school.[25] Used interchangeably with charismatic leadership,[26] or inspirational leadership,[27] transformational leadership is more than just charisma. It includes what Bass and Avolio referred to as the four I's—idealized influence (believing in the vision), inspirational motivation, intellectual stimulation, and individualized consideration.[28] Simply put, inspirational leaders are able to "elicit follower's internalized motivation" to carry out the leader's ideas and the organizational plan.[29] James McGregor Burns, the leading figure in developing transformational leadership, described the characteristics of transformational leaders this way:

> No leader can truly lead if he cannot respond to the wants of followers, if she fails to elevate and empower them. No leader can truly lead if lacking in the ability to produce intended change through creative innovation. No leader can lead without seeing that conflict is not only inevitable but often desirable; as Warren Bennis wrote, "exemplary corporate leaders not only accept dissent—they encourage and reward it. And leaders cannot be effective in the long run if they are simply power holders—rulers—and fail to see the moral and ethical implications of their work."[30]

One interesting development in leadership studies is derived from the work on emotional intelligence. In *Primal Leadership*, Goleman and others argue that leadership's main task is emotional. In their words, "this primordial emotional task, though by now largely invisible, remains foremost among the many jobs of leadership: driving the collective emotions in a positive direction and clearing the smog created by toxic emotions."[31] They identify resonant leaders as those who are in touch with their workers' emotions and feelings, explicitly emphasizing their importance:

> Roughly 50 to 70 percent of how employees perceive their organization's climate can be traced to the actions of one person: the leader. More than anyone else, the boss creates the conditions that directly determine people's ability to work well.[32]

Primal Leadership continues by providing an analysis of the emotionally intelligent leader with ideas for strengthening individual capacity toward becoming a more resonant leader, emphasizing the concomitant impact on organizational performance. Related research, termed as "emergent leadership," focuses on the managing of group emotion.[33]

The work on primal leadership is the latest in a long line of studies examining components of leaders and their work. Indeed, research on and theories about leadership are growth industries. There is no shortage of literature for the novice wanting to read about how to perform well when breaking into the upper organizational ranks. Theories abound with some well-researched studies, some "how-to" cookbooks, and some homespun remedies for leadership ills. Perhaps the best way to summarize the ever-growing body of research on leadership is to agree that leadership is more art than science. But, as Keith Grint has pointed out, this leaves us with four paradoxes that confuse its understanding.[34] First, the notion appears to have more to do with invention than analysis, despite claims to the contrary. Second, it appears to operate on the basis of indeterminacy while claiming to be deterministic. Third, it appears to be rooted in irony, rather than truth. Fourth, it usually rests on a constructed identity, but claims a reflective identity.

EMOTIONS IN THE WORKPLACE

A consistent theme in recent leadership studies is an acceptance that leadership is a human endeavor that has consequences. It is not coincidental that research on workplace emotions has experienced a dramatic shift of its own, especially within service-related industries. With this as the fastest growing labor market sector, it is no surprise that workplace emotion studies have been growing rapidly. As emotion researcher Neal Ashkanasy has suggested, "Cinderella" needs to be exposed to the limelight, with emotions included in organizational studies.[35] Or as Norwegian scholar Dorthe Eide concluded, "One may argue that it is high time that management and organizational scholars start including the everyday emotional life in their studies and theories . . . and then studying the many sides of emotions and not only seeing them as irrational."[36]

One confounding aspect of the literature on emotions is the difficulty in agreeing on what they are. The earliest attempts to define emotions can be traced back centuries. For example, Darwin's *The Expression of Emotions in Man and Animals*, first published in the 1870s, took an evolutionary perspective in describing what he considered as universal, basic emotions.[37] A decade later, psychologist William James posited a linear theory of emotions that progressed from perception, to arousal, to cognition.[38] But as modern emotion researchers have concluded, "defining emotions has continued to prove an elusive goal."[39] Kleinginna and Kleinginna found ninety-two definitions of emotions in the literature.[40] Concerning emotions theory, it has been said that, "there are as many theories about emotions as there are theorists."[41]

Our goal is not to find a precise definition or theory, nor to resolve the research community's conflicts. Instead, we want to emphasize what is known about emotions and how they can impact individuals in the workplace. Thus, Rolls recent definition that "emotions are states elicited by rewards or punishers" satisfies our need.[42] It is similar to the definition offered by Peter Salovey and John Mayer, who see emotions as "typically arising in response to an event, either internal or external, which has a positively or negatively valenced meaning for the individual."[43] In this sense, emotions are the resulting behavioral manifestations—either physical or psychological—from some real or perceived positive or negative interaction. Significantly, emotions are what one researcher described as the interface that mediates between environmental inputs and behavioral outputs.[44] They affect behavior and help make certain that an individual's or organization's needs are met. The experiential component is the key. To feel joy, or pain, or anger ignites some action, potentially impacting perceptions and feelings.[45] As the Norwegian researcher Arrne Naess wrote, "Emotions are not things that we own. They are some (-"thing") that originates in the meeting with ourselves-and-the-world."[46]

What the research teaches us is that there are many emotions. Robert Plutchik, a leading emotion researcher, posited eight primary emotions: joy, acceptance, fear, surprise, sadness, disgust, anger, and anticipation. Others have included shame and contempt.[47] Table 2.1 is an updated version of a table Matthews et al. presented based on Plutchik's work, with a few of our own additions based on our research. It lists typical emotions, a possible cause, thought process, and potential action each emotion might evoke. While a specific list identifying the basic emotions and their characteristics is debated constantly, it is clear that this list captures many of the core emotions that humans experience, their possible causes, and how they may impact our thinking and behavior.

Others have discussed secondary emotions: those emotions that have a strong cultural connection. As David Caruso explains, emotions like embarrassment are closely tied to cultural norms.[48] Secondary emotions evolve over one's lifetime, so a person's life experiences affect his development.[49]

These human emotions evolve over a lifetime, and development theorists have described how this evolution unfolds. Michael Lewis shows that infants are born with the capacity to have several emotions—like, anger, joy, surprise, sadness, disgust, and fear. The other range of emotions are acquired after two cognitive developments—the concept of the self and the acquisition of standards, rules, and goals (SRGs). These two developments permit the full range of adult emotions to emerge, as having a conception of self allows for emotions like embarrassment, envy, and empathy, while having SRGs allow for such emotions as embarrassment, pride, shame, and guilt.[50]

A key distinction that helps understand people's emotions is the difference drawn between emotions and mood. Emotions are short in duration and related to a specific stimulus or behavior. On the other hand, moods are something that last longer, aren't necessarily related to a specific stimulus, and are far more diffuse, often occurring for unknown reasons.[51] Moods may be ignited by experiencing emotions, and emotions are shorter and usually more

Table 2.1
Characteristics of Typical Emotions[a]

Typical Emotions	Possible Cause	Likely Thought Process	Potential Action
Fear, terror	A threat	Danger	Running away
Anger, rage	An obstacle	Enemy	Biting, hitting
Joy, ecstasy	Meeting a potential mate	Possessing	Courting, mating
Sadness, grief	A loss or death of a loved one	Isolation	Crying
Acceptance, trust	Becoming a group member	Friend	Grooming, sharing
Jealousy, envy	Losing a competition	Foe	Undermining, gossiping
Disgust, loathing	Seeing a gruesome object or heinous act	Poison	Vomiting, pushing away
Anticipation	Entering new territory (e.g., the first day of school)	What's out there?	Examining, mapping
Pride	An accomplishment	I did it!	Bragging
Surprise	Seeing a sudden novel object	What is it?	Stopping, alerting

[a] Derived and expanded from a table in G. Matthews, M. Zeidner, and R.D. Roberts, *Emotional Intelligence: Science and Myth*, 142. Cambridge: The MIT Press. Matthews et al. developed their table based on R. Plutchik, "A General Psychoevolutionary Theory of Emotion." *In Emotion: Theory Research and Experience*. Edited by R. Plutchik and H. Kellerman, 3-33. San Diego: Academic Press, 1980.

intense. In this conception, "affect" is the all-encompassing term that can refer to moods or emotions. While we are focusing on emotions throughout this book, lingering moods are also symptoms of some of the reactions we will be discussing about leaders.

One significant development on emotion research in organizational life is the work on emotional labor. Arlee Hochschild examined flight attendants and launched an avalanche of research while introducing the terms "emotional work" and "emotional labor."[52] Hochschild built on Erving Goffman's research depicting people as actors consciously managing their outer demeanor to conform to existing circumstances.[53] Hochschild argued that emotional work is the effort individuals put into keeping their private feelings suppressed or presented in socially acceptable ways. Emotional labor relates to wearing the organization's "mask" according to the accepted "display rules" for a particular organizational setting. Hochschild argued that employees use three strategies to manipulate their emotions: suppress genuine emotion, surface acting, or deep acting. Scholars have argued that emotional labor is experienced most strongly when individuals must express emotions that clash with their inner feelings. It is a viable reaction to the emotional dissonance experienced in the workplace.[54]

This notion of emotional labor is important as it can have profound consequences for individuals and organizations. In reviewing the literature one study identified three categories of possible outcomes.[55] The first was job-related attitudes and behaviors. Though these can be positive or negative, decreased job satisfaction and emotional overload are likely outcomes. The second category is physical and psychological well-being. Although emotional labor may help job performance, it impacts health and can lead to burnout. The final category is withdrawal behaviors. Sustained emotional dissonance with the requisite emotional labor that the job demands can lead to one withdrawing to escape the emotional burden.

The historical research on job-related stress and burnout is instructive here. Early research on stress built on the notion of the body's "flight or fight response," where negative emotions triggered by some threat or danger signal the body to prepare to defend and protect.[56] Stress researcher Hans Selye first defined stress as a nonspecific physiological response to various forms of harm, leading to feelings of anxiety or elevated heart rate.[57] Whatever the reaction, there is little dispute that stress has a dysfunctional impact on an individual. Researchers have identified six categories of factors that lead to job-related stress—factors intrinsic to the job, task, or workplace; role in the organization; problematic relationships with others at work; career development; organizational structure, climate, and culture; and the homework interface.[58] Chronic exposure to job stressors can result in burnout. Burnout is most common in those interacting with other people and is characterized by physical and emotional exhaustion, depersonalization or cynicism, and a low sense of personal accomplishment or job satisfaction.[59] Burnout can lead to impairing physical and emotional health or be the catalyst for someone quitting his or her job. Two studies done in 1990 suggested that stress and burnout were the cause of over 50 percent of employee absences and cost U.S. organizations about $150 billion a year due to lost days, reduced productivity, and medical costs.[60] One can only imagine the dollar figure today.

Thus, research tells us that emotions have a potent impact on an individual or business. Workplace situations and interactions can evoke emotions that

Table 2.2
Categories of Work-Related Emotions[a]

	More Adverse Effects	More Beneficial Effects
Job function-related	Boredom	Enjoyment
	Anxiety	Hope
	Indifference	Relief
	Despair	Pride
	Sadness	Confidence
	Insecurity	Accomplishment
	Shame/Guilt	
	Anger	
People-related	Social anxiety	Gratitude
	Embarrassment	Empathy
	Hate	Admiration
	Jealousy	Sympathy
	Contempt	Collegiality
	Fear	

[a] Derived and expanded from a table in G. Matthews, M. Zeidner, and R.D. Roberts, *Emotional Intelligence: Science and Myth,* 469. Cambridge: The MIT Press. Matthews et al. developed their table based on R. Pekrun and M. Frese, "Emotions in Work and Achievement," in *International Review of Industrial and Organizational Psychology,* 185. Eds. C.I. Cooper and I.T. Robertson. Chichester: John Wiley, 1992.

have been described along two dimensions.[61] The focus is either on the task at hand, what we refer to as job-function related, or social in nature, in our words: people-oriented. The particular emotions can be seen as having an adverse or beneficial impact. Table 2.2 displays these workplace emotions. This table builds on work that researchers who classify workplace emotions developed, with several additions we made based on our research and experiences.

Given both positive and negative emotions, it is clear that leaders need skill knowing what is happening emotionally with their employees. Without the ability to sense what is going on with their workers, leaders likely will have problems getting routine tasks accomplished. As two British psychologists have pointed out, emotions "serve to draw attention resources to issues that in some way threaten the individual integrity; whether that be physical, social, or psychological" and they "protect individuals from physical harm, facilitate the maintenance of self-identity in social settings, and guide the individual toward the achievement of tasks and goals."[62] Without the ability to grasp and act upon these effects of emotions on employees, leadership will be difficult.

Indeed, in highlighting the importance for leaders to understand emotions of others, David Caruso and Peter Salovey in *The Emotionally Intelligent Manager*,[63] provide a comparative list of skills that people may have for understanding emotions. They display these characteristics:

- Make correct assumptions about people.
- Know the right thing to say.
- Make good predictions about what people may feel.
- Have rich emotional vocabulary.
- Understand that one can feel conflicting emotions.
- Have sophisticated emotional knowledge.

People who aren't skillful in understanding emotions, however, display these characteristics:

- Misunderstand people.
- Get on people's nerves.
- Are surprised by how people feel.
- Find it hard to explain feelings.
- Experience on-or-off emotions with few shades of gray.
- Have only a basic understanding of emotions.

Obviously, the skilled and nonskilled differences are stark when it comes to understanding emotions. For leaders, the potential consequences in skill differences regarding emotional understanding are easy to discern and may certainly be dramatic.

Finally, having leaders understanding employee emotions becomes particularly poignant when it is clear that one's emotions can be conveyed to and even influence others. The concept of *emotional contagion* suggests that observing someone else's emotions has an impact. As one researcher put it, "through our interactions with other people, we catch their emotions."[64] Another study explained that leaders affect their employees through "subtle affective measures that are communicated outside of conscious awareness."[65] Yet another study described this as leaders infecting followers, with people mimicking others' facial expressions ultimately affecting their emotions.[66] Being around happy people can make you feel good, just as being with a depressed person can bring you down. Anger certainly has its repercussions. We all are aware that people tend to mimic others' emotions and expressions. The emotions we display, called *expressivity* by those who study this phenomenon, can impact everyone who surrounds a leader.[67] Dan Goleman and his colleagues sum up emotional contagion's significance for leaders very succinctly:

Everyone watches the boss: People take their emotional cues from the top. Even when the boss isn't highly visible . . . his attitude affects the moods of his direct reports, and a domino effect ripples throughout the company's emotional climate.[68]

INTELLIGENCE AND EMOTIONAL INTELLIGENCE

Intelligence is a construct that attempts to capture a broad set of abilities. Over time, the definition of intelligence has changed with the most cited definition of intelligence being Wechsler's statement that "intelligence is the aggregate or global capacity of the individual to act purposely, to think rationally, and to deal effectively with his environment."[69] E. L. Thorndike, an early intelligence researcher, first suggested the idea that there may be different types of intelligence. In 1920, in *Harper's Magazine*, Thorndike posited three modes of intelligence: abstract, mechanical, and social. Social intelligence was the ability to understand and manage people.[70] The controversy regarding social intelligence as a legitimate component of intelligence came from his son, R. L. Thorndike, who nearly twenty years after his father's comments wrote that little progress had been made understanding the concept.[71] Almost twenty-five years later, eminent Stanford researcher Lee Cronbach pronounced that research on the concept of social intelligence was fruitless.[72] Likely, this was the result of the inability to develop standardized measures encompassing real-life social situations.

Social intelligence remains controversial due to the difficulty in measuring the construct, distinguishing it from general intelligence, and concerns with finding validating criteria. That said, psychologists continue to study social intelligence, mostly concerned with the conceptual development of the topic.[73] Sternberg's related research on what he calls successful intelligences continues the tradition of social intelligence research.[74]

Gardner's widely popular work on multiple intelligences has related components to social intelligence.[75] Gardner's research includes what he refers to as personal intelligence, which encompasses interpersonal and intrapersonal intelligence. Interpersonal intelligence is the ability to understand the abilities, moods, and intentions of others. In Gardner's words:

Interpersonal intelligence builds on the core capacity to notice distinctions among others; in particular, contrasts in their moods, temperaments, motivations, and intentions. In more advanced forms, this intelligence permits a skilled adult to read the intentions and desires of others, even when these have been hidden.[76]

Intrapersonal is the more introspective intelligence. It involves the ability to access and discriminate among one's own feelings. Gardner explains intrapersonal intelligence as:

> Knowledge of the internal aspects of a person; access to one's own feeling life, one's range of emotions, the capacity to effect discriminations among these emotions and eventually to label them and to draw upon them as a means of understanding and guiding one's own behavior. A person with good intrapersonal intelligence has a viable and effective model of himself or herself.[77]

Dan Goleman's latest book is about social intelligence, which he describes as the new science of social relationships.[78] In recent years, debates about intelligence have been peppered with controversy as the concept of emotional intelligence has gained traction. Some see emotional intelligence as a nonvalidated concept caught up in a frenzy of media popularity, while others either see it as a natural component of overall intelligence or a separate domain worthy of independent status. The concept of emotional intelligence (EI) overlaps with Gardner's personal intelligences. The scholarship on EI has been both favorable and highly critical. Though popularized by Dan Goleman's bestselling book, *Emotional Intelligence*, John Mayer and Peter Salovey are credited with developing the original emotional intelligence construct. They define emotional intelligence this way:

> Emotional intelligence involves the ability to perceive accurately, appraise, and express emotion; the ability to access and/or generate feelings when they facilitate thought; the ability to understand emotion and emotional knowledge; and the ability to regulate emotions to promote emotional and intellectual growth.[79]

Others have proposed varying definitions, and a number of measures have evolved to assess emotional intelligence. The most popular are the Bar-on Emotional Quotient Inventory (EQ-i), The Emotional Competence Inventory (ECI), the Multi-Factor Emotional Intelligence Scale (MEIS), and most recently, the several versions of the Mayer, Salovey, Caruso Emotional Intelligence Test (MSCEIT).[80] Though these scales and tests differ, the four dimensions of EI measured by the scales developed by Mayer and his colleagues have gained wide acceptance. These include: the perception of emotion, the integration and assimilation of emotion, knowledge about emotions, and management of emotions. These are proposed as a sequence of steps. The third and fourth dimensions are particularly relevant for our interest in how managers deal with the emotional impact of their actions, as these dimensions involve how people understand their emotions, and the management of one's own emotions and those of others. But even with the measurement of EI, controversy is evident, as scholars suggest it is proving very difficult to accurately measure and that current scales are not particularly robust.[81]

The concept of EI is understandably appealing. It adds a dimension to account for successful performance heretofore ignored. Past research on job performance has documented that cognitive ability accounts for one quarter of the variance in job performance suggesting that there may be other concepts that may help us understand what makes a successfully performing leader.[82] Goleman's work has evoked the most reaction, as he has made controversial claims regarding the impact of EI, suggesting it is more significant for achieving success in life than intellectual intelligence. His work has spurred a great deal of interest, scholarship, and debate. He is assertive in his beliefs concerning the power of EI:

> In a sense we have two brains, two minds—and two different kinds of intelligence: rational and emotional. How we do in life is determined by both—it is not just IQ, but *emotional* intelligence that matters. Indeed, intellect cannot work at its best without emotional intelligence.[83]

This concept gives hope to all those with less than three-digit IQs (if you happen to know your number), and is a boon to those only hitting the fiftieth percentile on the SAT. No wonder the idea caught on like fire.

In the 1995 book *Emotional Intelligence,* Goleman implied that EI might predict up to 80 percent of your life's success. In a 1998 book, *Working with Emotional Intelligence,* he tempers this a bit, though he still argues that 67 percent of success at work can be predicted by EI.[84] And despite the scholarly controversy surrounding EI, there are defenders who are just as vigorous as the critics. Note the title of a recent article in the *Journal of Organizational Behavior,* "Rumors of the Death of Emotional Intelligence in Organizational Behavior Are Vastly Exaggerated."[85] More to the point, those working with leaders have jumped on EI as necessary for success, exemplified very succinctly in a recent article, appropriately titled, "Emotional Intelligence: The Key to Effective Performance."[86]

The most comprehensive analysis of EI comes in a recent book by Gerald Mathews, Moshe Zeidner, and Richard Roberts, *Emotional Intelligence: Science and Myth.*[87] They are more critical of the broad ideas proposed by Goleman, with his sweeping and largely unsubstantiated assertions like the

"old-fashioned word for the body of skills that emotional intelligence represents: character."[88] Noting that many of Goleman's concepts are too loose to
be considered science, they nonetheless hold out for a future where the concepts may be empirically testable and applaud Goleman's work as a source
of ideas. While they identify impediments to the progress of research on EI
and seek to debunk the many myths that have been associated with it, they
are supportive of the more scientific research underway by leaders like John
Mayer, Peter Salovey, and Reuven Bar-On. They conclude with this appraisal
and somewhat optimistic assessment:

> Emotional intelligence has caught the imagination of the general pub-
> lic, the commercial world, and the scientific community. It matches
> the current zeitgeist of self-awareness and understanding, redressing
> a perceived imbalance between intellect and emotion in the life of the
> collective Western mind. Emotional intelligence also connects with sev-
> eral cutting-edge areas of psychological science, including the neuron-
> science of emotion, self-regulation theory, studies of meta cognition, and
> the search for human cognitive abilities beyond traditional academic in-
> telligence.
>
> The supposed malleability of emotional intelligence has consider-
> able appeal to practitioners tackling personal and social problems. It is
> perceived as a panacea for clinical patients locked into private misery;
> obstructive, unproductive employees; and violent, antisocial children.
> Beyond the more dramatic manifestations of emotional illiteracy, many
> essentially adjusted people feel their lives would benefit from greater
> skills in understanding their own emotions and those of other people.[89]

The lack of precision in the conceptualization of EI, along with concerns
regarding the objectivity of the construct, are two areas that scholars will address in the future. Due to its attractiveness to the lay public and mental health
practitioners, it is likely that EI will continue to grow in popularity. Certainly
there are differences in how well individuals perceive, understand, and deal
with emotions, and there are skills that can be learned to help people to grow
in these areas. But even EI researcher Peter Mayer calls for restraint in considering its potential:

> Popular claims, such as that emotional intelligence is "twice as impor-
> tant" as traditional intelligence in predicting success, seem overblown,
> no matter how they are interpreted. Traditional personality research
> on what contributes to success is far more informative in this regard

than popular accounts of the new area of emotional intelligence. Current research on emotional intelligence measured as an ability, however, does suggest that it may predict—at modest levels—important outcomes such as reduced rates of problem behaviors.[90]

Despite such cautions, EI has taken on a life of its own over the past fifteen years. In the leadership literature, a spin-off of EI has come of age in the work of Robert Cooper and Ayman Sawaf. In their book, *Executive EQ: Emotional Intelligence in Leadership and Organizations*,[91] they suggest that emotional intelligence, what they call EQ, will be the driving force for the twenty-first century, as IQ accounts for less than 10 percent of real-world success. So they offer a four-cornerstone model of EQ, including what they call emotional literacy, emotional fitness, emotional depth, and emotional alchemy. The book is replete with an EQ questionnaire (the EQ Map), scoring grid, and interpretation guide to help managers calculate where they are weak and strong in elements of EQ. As discussed in the section on leadership, Goleman, too, has connected his work to the leadership world, arguing that self-awareness, self-regulation, motivation, empathy, and social skill, the five components of emotional intelligence, are powerful predictors of leader success. His conclusions, reported in the *Harvard Business Review*, were quite stark:

> Moreover, my analysis showed that emotional intelligence played an increasingly important role at the highest levels of the company, where differences in technical skills are of negligible importance. In other words, the higher the rank of a person considered to be a star performer, the more emotional intelligence capabilities showed up as the reason for his or her effectiveness. When I compared star performers with average ones in senior leadership, nearly 90% of the difference in their profiles was attributable to emotional intelligence factors rather than cognitive abilities.[92]

Excitement about work on emotional intelligence is inevitable when the concept is presented as it is given the prevalence in our culture of holding such a premium on success. Stephen Covey has created an industry around promoting the habits of effective people.[93] We all want to be successful. Success, of course, is a very individually defined concept, though it is discussed with great regularity in the popular media. Sometimes simple measures are used, like academic achievement for youth or performance or income for adults. Other times the definition is more complex. In one study examining the vocational success of adults with learning disabilities, success was defined along five dimensions—income, job classification, job-related reputation or eminence, education level, and job satisfaction. This research drew its definition from a review of the literature that suggested that success includes both objective and subjective components. The authors concluded:

> Any study focusing on success faces the difficult challenge of defining the term. What at first may appear to be a routine research-related process of identifying, defining, and operationalizing a variable quickly evolves into a much more onerous task. Why? Because success is in the eyes of the beholder. Whereas making a great deal of money may signal success for some, enjoying one's work, working for a prestigious company, or having a happy and healthy family may be more important for others.[94]

The variability in definitions of success is obvious when examining other studies. Some projects involve interviews with managers to identify characteristics associated with success and failure. Success dimensions examined include emotional stability and composure, lack of defensiveness, interpersonal skills, and technical-cognitive skills.[95] A number of studies look at progression within an organizational hierarchy as the measure of success, what one set of writers refer to as the rate of advancement (ROA).[96] What is clear is that although the definition of success is very subjective and certainly a personal matter, it is a term used as a dependent measure in many studies associated with leadership, emotions, and emotional intelligence.

TYING IT ALL TOGETHER

The literature we've examined concerns leadership, emotions, intelligence, and emotional intelligence. Today it is clear that emotions are being acknowledged in organizational behavior and leadership studies, though a great deal of murkiness and controversy clouds these disparate fields. For too many scholars, however, emotions remain a taboo arena and even the highly recognized concept of emotional intelligence is dismissed by many as nonscientific. In the popular leadership press, being emotional has come to be seen as significant for organizational success, most prominently reflected in the work of Thomas Peters and Nancy Austin,[97] who see workplace emotions and feelings as necessary ingredients for managerial success. Peters, for example, urged leaders to be enthusiastic about the products of the company, suggesting that they even laugh, cry, and smile in order to be effective.[98]

Other studies have focused on a number of other leadership issues related to emotions. For example, the importance of intuition in organizational management has been emphasized,[99] as have nonscientific nonlogical processes that aid in managerial success.[100] Indeed, in Chester Barnard's early seminal work on leadership in the 1930s, he recognized that leaders' emotions could impact their behavior. He suggested that when an executive's moral code faces conflict, the result might be emotional feelings potentially leading to paralysis.[101] About twenty years later, Robert Katz argued that performance of effective leaders depended on three things: technical skill, conceptual skill, and human skill. Human skill, he explained, is "the way the individual perceives (and recognizes the perceptions of) his superiors, equals, and subordinates, and the way he behaves subsequently."[102]

Related to research on human feelings and skills, organizational and leader behavior studies have suggested that what may be considered people's background and temperament have an impact on behavior. Such studies relied on psychodynamic Freudian-style theories to explain corporate culture and behavior. One study argued that organizations are not shaped solely by their environments, but also by "the unconscious concerns of their members and the unconscious forces shaping the societies in which they exist."[103] Another, in discussing research on leaders and managers, asked, "To what extent do repressed, 'unresolved' early-life emotional struggles re-emerge in the organizational forms they create?"[104] This study goes on to show how the work of leaders like Frederick Taylor and Henry Ford were shaped by their background and temperament.

But even while recognizing the importance that background and human skills play in organizational behavior, the research has generally ignored the specific impact that emotions can play on individuals in leadership roles. Stephen Fineman explained this shortcoming thus: "the student of work organizations would find little in existing organizational theory to reveal the detail of such phenomena [emotions], despite an enormous shift from a strictly rationalistic view of organizations. . . . We find little or no mention of how feeling individuals worry, envy, brood, become bored, play, despair, plot, hate, and so forth."[105] Similarly, Iain L. Mangham argued that this lack of attention to emotions is directly related to the generally accepted sense that studying things like "feelings" has no place in organizational research. He explained it this way:

The general neglect of emotions by contemporary writers on behaviour in organizations seems largely due to an acceptance of the common managerial perception that "feelings" (a term often used pejoratively) have no place in institutions that are committed to considering judgment and rational action. They get in the way and cloud the issues.[106]

The bulk of related research, therefore, only recently began to include emotions in studies on leadership and organizational behavior in any meaningful way. Heretofore the research has either ignored the impact of emotions on organizational or leader behavior or simply suggested that behaving in specified emotional ways is an ingredient affecting success. Being enthusiastic and motivating, being emotional to spur on the staff, were the ways that emotions entered discussions about leadership. More recently, research has emerged on the importance of EI for individual behavior and success. However, even this work doesn't specifically examine the impact that emotional experiences have on those in leadership roles. In fact, most of the research has had a very top-down orientation, focusing on how leaders affect those that work for them. But little research has taken the alternate perspective that emotions can have a bottom-up impact as well, affecting leaders in a variety of ways. In the next few chapters we will begin to explore these shortcomings through the stories from those in leadership positions in business, schools, community colleges, and universities.

CHAPTER 3

The Eye of the Storm: The Agony of Decision Making

As anyone who has lived in the southeast United States knows, hurricanes are circular structures around an eerily calm eye. As a hurricane passes through, we experience the storm, then the calm, and then the storm again. I write this account from the eye of the hurricane.

—president of a community college

We were at a conference a few years ago and met Don, who discussed his years as an executive working for a major computer hardware and parts manufacturer. The company had plants all over the world, but the plant where he served as the senior executive was one of their largest. As plant manager, he was a prominent community person since the plant was the town's leading employer. He served on numerous boards and was involved with several community development projects. He had grown up in the company and moved up their corporate ladder to his present leadership role. As he told us, "thirty years with one company is a long time." But until he jumped into senior leadership they had been good years. He had been relocated to company plants throughout the United States and Europe. He assured us that the company had a reputation for treating employees well, an industry approach he called, "their way," and he always had been proud to be associated with the manufacturer.

Don was a very personable guy, and people really liked him. Most leadership team members were longtime friends; he had coaxed several to join him when he took on this leadership role. But the last few years had been agonizing for him. High-tech industry changes centering on Hammer and Champy's "reengineering" had changed the way the company operated.[1] Don lamented numerous layoffs and changes that tore at his heartstrings. He was pleased that the company had fairly generous severance policies, but even these were reduced when the high-tech bubble burst. He explained how he had hated trimming his budget and cutting corners to save money, sensing that layoffs were always around the corner. Even very profitable plant sectors were at risk. The employees, many high-priced engineers, were on edge as well. When cuts came, as they did in several waves, they were devastating to him, to those affected, and to the health of the community he had come to love.

Don explained that he felt it was his responsibility to face employees one-on-one when they were being laid off. It was time-consuming, but at least he could explain that the decision wasn't related to their performance. In some instances highly regarded and profitable divisions were eliminated because they weren't seen as fitting the corporate direction. In describing the sensation he felt when dismissing his lifelong friends and others he personally had hired, he used the word "excruciating" over and over again. "How do you tell someone who has several kids in college," he asked, "that they are out of a job?" What do you say to them when they question the decision and point to the good work they had been doing? Once he had to tell a young woman who was pregnant that she was being let go because the company was changing its direction. Another time he had to face a friend whose wife recently had been diagnosed with cancer and explain that his services were no longer needed. "All my care and passion when talking to these good people wouldn't pay their bills," he told us. "Thankfully we kept them on their insurance for a year." But even this was little solace to him, knowing that the job picture was bleak for anyone in this field. And the meetings he described with community leaders were tense and hard on him. He kept up the corporate face and assured everyone that everything would be fine, but his insides suggested this optimism was not well-founded.

Then, after thirty years with the company, Don was eventually let go as the company's downturn and revamping continued. The entire plant was being downsized. Now he had to go back to his community friends and share the devastating news that their worst fears would be realized. This was especially unnerving to him because he had been told again and again that this plant was "safe." Based on those assurances he had assured local leaders that he and the plant would be around a long time. Now he had to go back on his word. It made him look bad and he hurt.

Some employees were offered positions elsewhere, but at his level and salary that was impossible unless he was willing to take a significant cut in pay, responsibilities, and relocate. At least, he said, his community friends who were livid at the company felt some compassion for him losing his job after so many years. Don told us,

> You know, as much as I hated making cuts and dismissing people who were good at what they did, I got a weird sense of satisfaction and pleasure watching my boss's face as he let me go. He was squirming in his chair as much as I used to when performing the same task. We both agreed that the company culture had changed, and he shared that letting me go was the most excruciating task he had ever undertaken. I absolutely knew what he was feeling.

As Don's saga suggests, being a leader can at times make you feel that you are in the eye of a storm. The first wave comes racing across your desk demanding immediate action. You satisfy its demands and are met by an eerie silence you are afraid to trust. Then you hear the rush and the backside of the storm comes howling through your office. We don't want to overdramatize this notion and suggest that life as leader is always bad or that hard decisions affect everyone the same way. We are all wired differently, and leaders have varying capacities for dealing with the effects of the decisions they make and acts they must perform. We also realize that decisions we all make in everyday life can be very difficult and traumatic. This was brought home to us in a story we recently read about a young couple whose son, though apparently healthy and very bright, had a seizure disorder. Their options included a costly and dangerous brain surgery with a 75 percent survival rate that would possibly stop the seizures but leave the child in a wheelchair. Then there was the option to do nothing and watch his cognitive ability deteriorate until he would eventually die before he reached age thirty. The parents explained that they decided to take the risk, though the decision had been the most agonizing they ever experienced. Being a leader in any capacity involves making difficult decisions.

Decisions that leaders make may be for short-term or long-term direction and include a wide variety of organizational issues. Every year leaders decide raises, bonuses, and fringe packages for their employees. Budget-related considerations, promotions, hiring and retention decisions, all are leadership activities. Making decisions is the job. Research on being a principal, for example, highlights that each day there are numerous decisions that require very quick responses.[2] These responses and decisions fall to the leader, heightening the emotional reaction when others are affected. A middle-sized company executive laughed and explained how his employees always say how hard his job is, but, they inevitably tell him, "that is why you make the big bucks!"

He wondered aloud if the extra compensation really was worth the added responsibility, pressure, and emotional fallout that follows tough decisions.

To better understand the impact decision making has on leaders, we collected formal stories from leaders in school districts, community colleges, and four-year universities.[3] Subsequently, we held follow-up conversations and collected stories from business executives. We were interested in two related matters. First, what decisions evoke the strongest emotional response from leaders? Second, how did leaders react to decisions that aroused an emotional response from them?

DECISIONS THAT EVOKE STRONG EMOTIONS

What we found didn't surprise us. The decisions that generated the strongest emotional response were those related to personnel matters. Two-thirds of our participants described a personnel situation related to employee reassignment, dismissal, or release. In some instances, the leaders described decisions related to reassignment or a yearly evaluation that caused the pain. Though the specifics that instigated the need for this personnel action differed, the most common causes were incompatibility between employee and responsibilities or budget cutbacks and financial exigencies. Other difficult decisions affecting leaders included employees disobeying rules, sexual harassment conflicts, and unacceptable job performance. Interestingly, in 25 percent of these cases, the person being terminated or reassigned was the leader's close personal friend. This is an issue we delve into more deeply in the next chapter.

These personnel-related matters were emotional experiences for the leaders, and their stories highlighted their concerns for people with whom they worked as the basis for the dissonance that the experience engendered. Thus, they experienced anxiety when dealing with a colleague, even when his or her performance was unacceptable and deserving of critical response. This anxiety was caused by the financial, personal, and career impact that the leader's decision would cause. We heard the leaders proclaim their dislike for the yearly evaluation system their organization utilized. "Everyone seems to think they are the lead-off hitter, a key for the success of the company," one business leader explained to us. "But how do you tell someone who has worked his or her buns off that the raise is far lower than he or she expected?" One dean at a middle-sized university said that given the small percentages available for raises, she would dump the merit system and just give across the board raises. "Recognizing merit is important," she said. "But the process is far too much work for the dollars involved, and except for a small minority, everyone is disappointed and gets angry about it. But guess who gets blamed?" A small construction company owner told us, "It's always hard to face someone and tell them they aren't worth what they think they are, even if the person is weak and deserves to be fired."[4]

The other issues causing leaders an emotional reaction involved dealing with a tragedy (e.g., a shooting on the premises), leadership-style conflicts, making sweeping changes, and on-the-job dishonesty. However, these issues all shared a common ingredient with the personnel-related stories. We label this emerging idea as the "human toll" that emotionally laden experiences had on these leaders. In other words, since leadership involves daily human-to-human contact, it was a direct result of the person-to-person interactions that caused the emotional responses the leaders shared. It wasn't about bricks and mortar, strategic planning, working on a project or activity that caused pain; but rather it was the decisions affecting coworkers that created leaders' anxiety and took its "human toll." In the course of doing their jobs the leaders were exposed to numerous situations that had required them to make decisions affecting their employees. These were the actions that kept them up at night.

REACTIONS TO DECISIONS: FEELING THE AGONY

When we analyzed our stories and interviews to better understand how leaders cope with their decisions affecting their coworkers, the notion of the "human toll" became clearer. In fact, we labeled the response that the leaders discussed as the *"agony of decision-making."* Leader after leader described situations that they found difficult to navigate. We also found that many leaders hid their emotions, and displayed a *"corporate face"* to appear confident and stable before their colleagues. But this had an emotional toll as well.

The agony of decision making was evident in every story these leaders shared. We discuss several stories we heard to show how leaders expressed considerable anxiety related to the circumstances surrounding their decisions and the actions they took. Some leaders were new to their positions and were concerned about the impact their decisions might have. Others reacted to the effects of changes they were promoting. Most commonly there was anxiety concerning the effects their decision would have on others' lives. But no matter the intervening variables, the leaders discussed their deeply felt emotions, sleepless nights, and high anxiety levels. They cared about their work, their employees, and the impact their decisions had on everyone.

One notable story involved a college president who was distressed at cutbacks she was forced to undertake. It wasn't that the decision was wrong.

Rather, the concern was for the people she would impact. Dr. Francisco was new to her job as a small college president. A presidency was something she had spent "a lifetime preparing for," and the new job was the capstone of her highly successful career. Having achieved her ultimate goal, she was dismayed to be thrust into a situation demanding severe cuts. But making the cuts was ultimately the right decision. Her board was behind her, but she faced the unfortunate task of explaining the plan to the faculty and staff. She knew it wouldn't be easy, but she was taken back at how hard it was for her.

The college had been operating inefficiently for years. Losses were hidden and mounting, while programs were being expanded. Dr. Francisco told us "it was nuts." The entire operation was built on an inefficient and inequitable formula, though few at the college, most notably the faculty, were aware of how inequitably they had been treated and how much in debt they really were. As she described the situation to us, we now see it as sharing many elements that led to Enron's downfall, though it lacked Enron's purposeful cooking of the books and individual financial gains. Dr. Francisco knew that she was well-trained and capable of devising and implementing a plan for cutbacks. But she never fully appreciated the emotional intensity she would experience until she actually implemented the plan.

Dr. Francisco created a retrenchment model and process that was collaborative. She believed in sharing information and arranged meetings to explain the situation and the process. She told us, "I am in the middle of this excruciating process, dismantling pieces of the college, perhaps risking the position to which I aspired for so long." Though she knew what she was doing was necessary and would be best for the college's future, it didn't diminish the pain she felt. She worked day and night, planning and thinking through the best way to approach the dilemma. She bounced ideas off friends and colleagues whom she could trust to be discreet. When the time came she shared the circumstances and plan with her administrative team. Some would be affected directly, and perhaps demoted or released. Their shocked expressions troubled her. But she persisted.

Dr. Francisco told us that the emotional pain she felt throughout this ordeal caught her off guard. After all, she had held positions of authority, had made hard decisions, and had experienced the emotions they evoked. But somehow, she hadn't prepared herself for the emotional fallout that a president receives. This was different. It was all on her. She obsessed about what to do and how to approach this. "For several weeks I tossed and turned at night, rising to make notes to myself about points I should make, people to whom I needed to talk. I just couldn't escape the heaviness of heart. I exercised each morning, tried to take care of myself, but I talked less about my work with my husband, as I was just emotionally spent."

Dr. Francisco's story illustrates what leaders told us across a wide spectrum of businesses, industries, and organizations. The emotional pain transcended gender and years of leadership experience. When leaders make decisions that directly affect and possibly harm people, it is very difficult for them to accept. For some it resulted in sleepless nights. Others said they could fall asleep, but found themselves soon awake unable to get back to bed. Like Dr. Francisco, they obsessed, got up to make notes, and couldn't relax. One Dean told us, "my heart gets to racing, and I just know that I'm not getting anymore sleep that night. So I get up and work and get more anxious." Other leaders experienced nervous stomachs, irritability, and other classic signs of being overly stressed or burned out.[5]

Interestingly, another college president faced much the same situation as Dr. Francisco. In this case, Dr. Dettwiler was in his second presidency, had experienced cutbacks, organizational redesigns, strategic planning processes, and knew full well what to expect when times got tough. Yet that didn't diminish the pain he felt in implementing a plan his board handed him soon after he assumed his new position. As Dr. Dettwiler explained, his board told him that with state budget cuts, declining enrollments, increased costs for utilities, and union contracts, there needed to be a reduction in faculty. He agreed the need was real but that didn't diminish the anguish he experienced. He had to get over the self-anger he felt for not evaluating his new situation more accurately before he signed the contract. The new retrenchment policy was to be presented to the campus beginning fall semester. He felt lonely knowing what was about to unfold, and very disturbed by what he knew would follow. As he explained,

> For me, I was in a state of higher anxiety. I knew I had started a process that was now beyond my power to stop. I bore the responsibility but none of the control. I took long walks at night to try to unwind and sleep. I couldn't confide in anyone on campus, and I was too new to the state to have established a support network among the other community college presidents. I remember being gripped by my own fears: for faculty who would have to be released, for their families, for the college's community image, and in all honesty, for my own professional position. Could I, would I be made the scapegoat for this problem?

Of course, it isn't only in academia that leaders experience this distress. A construction company CEO told us how hard it is for him to deal with employees he hired. His business was family to him, and he hoped that everyone else felt the same way. The company had grown quickly and was managing projects all over the country. But their business was project-driven, and there were periods when some people had to be let go. It got so hard for him that he hired someone, "to do his dirty work for him." That didn't diminish his pain, "but at least I didn't have to look them in the eye knowing the problems this might cause for them."

One last story illustrates the consistent theme the leaders described to us. A superintendent from a moderate-sized school district in a Western state shared an incident involving his district's students. School superintendents work at the pleasure of the Board of Education in every school district in the United States. It takes a majority vote of one to dismiss a superintendent, though they do work on a contractual basis. Many superintendents who get crosswise with their school board negotiate a contract settlement and resign to pursue other positions. Ironically, this can have financial benefits if the superintendent lands another position. The same phenomenon is true in the world of professional and high-profile college sports, where coaches (managers in baseball), are routinely dismissed before a contract expires and are paid for not working. Finding another job may mean having two salaries. However, being dismissed or being forced to resign from a position can put a "stain" on a professional resume, but more important, no leader likes to admit failure in anything she or he does.

Dr. Wallpoll and his board clashed over ethics, not his failure. He felt his board was making decisions that were bad for children. Though he was tentative about providing many specifics, he did say that the board made decisions that were wrong because they were harmful to kids. He knew that it was his job to carry out the directives the board handed him, but he felt as if his gut were in a "vice." Should he ignore the board "and do what was right for the children?" Or should he honor the contractual and reporting relationship and implement the board's decisions as gently as possible?

Years ago, political scientist Albert O. Hirschman wrote a book called *Exit, Voice, and Loyalty*.[6] In it he explained that members of businesses, other organizations, and the polity have essentially three choices in dealing with policies that negatively affect them. They can leave the community (exit); they can complain and try to make the required actions conform more closely to their wishes (voice); or they can accept the decisions and move on with their lives (loyalty). For Dr. Wallpoll, this was a particularly stressful situation and the choices before him all involved emotional trade-offs. His family had been uprooted when he accepted the superintendency, and they didn't want to move again, because the community had become home for him and his family. So, exiting was an awful choice as there was no likely position for him either with the school district or in this particular community that would meet his personal and financial needs.

He continued to express his concerns to the board; they were respectful but simply disagreed with him. Perhaps they were concerned about the financial impact on the budget if they agreed to what he described as "doing the right thing," but Dr. Wallpoll didn't believe that was the case. So he had tried the "voice" option, but to no avail. That left the idea of just carrying out the board's wishes, the "loyalty" option, or leaving ("exit"). He started to implement the loyalty option, but he just "couldn't do what they wanted and look at himself in the mirror each morning." So he decided to try once more to convince the board to change paths to take the right action for the kids. The majority ignored his pleas, but one member said that if he didn't like it, he could look for another job. This made the next step obvious to him, but he still agonized over the impact on the district's kids. Note his description of the situation:

> After this brief discussion with the board chairman, I realized that there was absolutely no reason for me to stay. . . . I went back to my office and prepared a resignation. I had no job in mind, but I knew I could no longer work in this district with its board of education. They had violated every principle I knew in protecting children. I was emotionally spent mostly because of what happened to these kids. Now, I had no relationship with the board, and I had no job. This was a very difficult emotional time worrying about finding a job on such short notice and what was going to happen to these poor children that had been betrayed. . . . As I write this story the emotions flood back into my head, my heart and my gut, and the nauseating truth of what happened in that district will always remain with me. I am a Vietnam veteran who saw my share of misery and suffering, but those experiences, no matter how awful they were, don't compare to the disgusting feelings I still have about this incident.

Imagine that. The emotional stress he experienced as the school district's leader surpassed the horrors he experienced as a soldier on the Vietnam battlefields. Researchers studying stress have shown that inner-city school teachers often displayed higher stress levels than pilots who flew wartime missions, probably because the pilots were better prepared for the emotional side of flying wartime combat.[7] Many leaders, it appears, are as ill prepared as inner-city teachers for dealing with the emotional situations they will face on the job. The emotional depth and intensity these leaders described were dramatic. Characterizing the emotions and pain felt in a school-related incident to the misery witnessed in the Vietnam War is telling. Being a leader and making difficult decisions can cause tremendous pressure and agony.

REACTIONS TO DECISIONS: THE RIGHT FACE

There is another side to the agony of decision making that leaders shared. We refer to it as *showing the right face*. As we discussed in the previous chapter, there is a growing literature on what Hochschild first referred to as emotional work and emotional labor.[8] The "work" is the effort required to keep emotions under control, while the "labor" refers to displaying the right behavior for the setting in which one is employed. What some have referred to as wearing the company "mask," and others as "deep acting," all refer to the sorts of "display rules" that govern being in charge.[9] Leaders are perceived to have to behave in a certain way, as they conceive their role being governed by rules that preclude displaying workplace emotions. Grandey explained that research on this emotional work suggests that although the emotional labor can have positive effects on an organization's performance, it also can have negative effects on one's health. Indeed, research shows that health and psychological well-being and adjustment can be affected.[10] Though these studies aren't generally focused on the emotional labor attached to being a leader, it certainly follows that wearing the company mask when confronted with emotional circumstances can affect a leader's well-being. The stories we heard certainly underscored this reality.

What we learned was that some leaders felt it necessary to present themselves in a particular way to maintain organizational health and convey their stature as the leader. One leader related a particularly telling story confronting a workplace crisis. Mary had been president for several years. There had been an accident and some people were killed. Friends had lost friends; families were torn apart—it was devastating. But Mary felt it necessary to present a strong image to the workers to get everyone through the crisis. It was hard on her. Following the 9/11 tragedy in New York City, both Mayor Giuliani and President Bush earned high marks for their strength in the wake of the tragic terrorist acts. But for Mary, the losses were all friends or people she had known. The pain was closer than that with which the politicians deal. Mary described her approach this way:

There is no question that I felt great grief during this situation, but a president must find private time for these emotions . . . in this situation,

one must steel oneself, because you must act on behalf of others, making
sure of their well being and safety. You cannot do this if you abdicate
your leadership by indulging your emotions. If and when you decide to
fall apart, you must do it someplace else, and later on. People need to
know that whoever the leader is, he or she is operating from a position
of strength. When they lose that confidence, where can they turn? So I
think the leader must be steadfast, must be strong.

Obviously, this wasn't easy for Mary. But she felt that her job required what
might be described as a superhuman response to crisis. She wore the "mask"
that she felt was appropriate to help the company. The particular toll that it
might have on her was deemed secondary to the role expectations she had for
herself.

One might argue that a crisis like the one Mary confronted required a
Giuliani and Bush-like attitude to help everyone get through the unthinkable.
Leaders must put their own emotions aside and be the mother- or fatherlike
figure that people look to in crisis. While we know of no evidence to support this assertion, does it also hold, then, that leaders must display a certain
face no matter what the circumstances? One college president we talked to
described a period of cutbacks where legal parameters and the college's attor-
neys governed his behavior. Dr. Batcher felt so constrained in what he could
share and the behaviors he could display to the college community that it was
driving him crazy. In his mind, a little more emotion would have better served
the college. But he was a "company man" and followed the lawyers' dictates.
It was terribly discomforting to him. In Dr. Batcher's words:

I think back on it and the whole approach makes me physically and
emotionally sick again. The faculty returned in the fall, and I laid out
for them what we had accomplished in the summer. I promised that we
would go to each division and present our findings so that every faculty
member would know exactly where his or her division and department
stood and to show how the criteria were applied to everyone in a full
time faculty line. No one was exempt from the process. . . . I was walking
the line between the feelings and compassion for the individuals, and
the lawyers telling me what I could and could not say, could and could
not do. It didn't turn out as I or anyone hoped, and the final outcome
was worse than even I expected.

The emotional work these two leaders had to go through was immense.
In the first instance, Mary would have loved to just cry her eyes out in front

of everyone as she told us that really would have been a better representation of how she felt. In the other story, Dr. Batcher described the "aching feeling" he couldn't get rid of during the entire retrenchment process. He wanted to "point to the idiots in charge" and yell and scream just as the employees were doing to him. But that wasn't the way he was allowed to behave, and he acted accordingly. These leaders weren't passionless ogres as many may have portrayed them. They felt their employees' pain. But as leaders, they comported themselves so as to be seen as strong. And being seen as strong meant not showing emotions to those in their charge. These leaders presented themselves in ways that they felt were in the organization's best interest. Researchers have shown that this emotional labor can cause great distress when the emotional face one must present conflicts with one's innermost feelings.[11] While we didn't perform any sort of health-related checkups, we would guess that both Mary and Dr. Batcher and a number of others to whom we spoke, were experiencing some problems. Showing the right face is demanding work.

The decisions leaders make and the ways they often behave can have a heavy personal toll. What we call the "agony of decision-making" tries to capture the effects that leaders experience making difficult decisions. You don't have to be your organization's CEO to experience these leadership travails. Very often it is the unit or department leader who is the closest to the actual event and must respond quickly through the emotional haze. What we haven't discussed yet are two instances that are particularly challenging for leaders. These include dealing with employees who are especially difficult, and making decisions that directly impact friends. We turn to these specific matters in the next chapter.

CHAPTER 4

Extra Grace Required

I work really hard to make Ed happy. I give him what he wants, am always fair and cordial even when he is nasty and passive-aggressive; nothing seems to make a difference. He still undermines me at every turn. I can't please him; I can't control him; and I am at wits-end trying to figure out what to do next. It literally is driving me crazy. I know it bothers me more than it should. All too often I find myself playing back our interactions. I keep wondering if I should have said something differently. I just don't get it. If I ever say anything about him to anyone else they look at me like I'm crazy. "Ed, you must just misunderstand him. He's a great guy." But he's not. He's a jerk, he doesn't treat people very nicely whom he sees as his inferiors, and he's a drain on me and the department. Everyone else is clueless about how this guy acts and how destructive he is being. I just can't seem to let it go.

—university administrator

A friend recently was telling a story about his church work. He and the minister were discussing some parishioners. Some always were being very difficult; they demanded a great deal yet contributed little. The minister described them as being "in need of extra grace." It turns out that "extra grace required" is a fairly common Christian church concept. It describes individuals needing special grace and care. Reverend Andrew D. Burns described the term this way:

The world is full of people with unhealed wounds, deep insecurities, irritating mannerisms, poor social skills, and dysfunctional backgrounds. They are EGR people—Extra Grace Required!

Every Church has them, every landlord has them, every employer has them...the folks that we wonder "How does God put up with them?...I know I sure can't stand 'em!"[1]

An antiabortion group working with women having unplanned pregnancies had an article in their newsletter called "When You Feel Like Giving Up on Someone." The author, a pastor from Massachusetts, wrote: "One seminar speaker referred to them as 'EGR' people, *extra grace required*. When you deal with EGR people, you need special reserves of God's grace. They may be irresponsible, critical, abusive, and manipulative. They seldom follow through on plans. They fail to show up for appointments. Sadly, some appear to reject all we say.... We have all met such people. They make you want to give up..."[2]

WORKING WITH DIFFICULT EMPLOYEES

How does this relate to the work world most leaders face? We heard several stories about what one University leader called his "high maintenance faculty member," whose behavior was very similar to the EGR person church groups describe. These high maintenance types are demanding, resistant to anything suggested, nasty, critical, and abusive. They ignore any suggestions offered concerning their performance and routinely dismiss meetings or job expectations they consider unimportant or inconvenient. They require special treatment and care to weave their potential into the organization's work. Many never change their behavior and are an ongoing discomfort to the leader. Such people require "extra grace." Every reader could describe these individuals. You agonize over meeting with them. When you see them on your calendar, you hope that something else comes up so you can cancel. Every interaction is a battle. They challenge you every opportunity they have. For the leaders we talked to these individuals created continual tension and stress.

Of course, difficult employees don't just affect leaders. Indeed, Robert Sutton, a management science and engineering professor at Stanford University, recently wrote a book about the impact of working with these EGR types. He very vividly titled the book *The No Asshole Rule: Building a Civilized Workplace and Surviving One That Isn't*.[3] He poignantly emphasizes the negative effects and costs such people bring to their organization—to the victims, bystanders, and overall performance—and offers a set of tips for surviving such people.

But for our leaders, the stories we heard brought to mind a chapter from a book by dog trainer Barbara Woodhouse, *No Bad Dogs*.[4] Ms. Woodhouse argues that dog owners were really the culprit when a dog wasn't well behaved, and the dog trainer's real task was to train the owner. She did warn, however, that there were some dogs that possibly were unbalanced psychologically, or they were mistreated as pups, but for whatever reason, were untrainable. Much like these animals the "high maintenance—EGR" employees never were going to conform to the institutional norms or the leader's expectations. Nothing anyone did was going to change them. Their paranoiac ways are set thinking leaders are out to get them. They soak up time and energy and are emotionally draining. They clearly need extra grace.

One Dean described his EGR faculty member very clearly. "Every year, like clockwork, I can count on a nasty response to his evaluation and a grievance after I turn down his absurd demands. It's as predictable as death and taxes, and there isn't any action legal or otherwise that I can take to counter this behavior." Leaders shared stories that made us realize that every organization has employees who are demanding, narcissistic, and unwilling to see beyond their personal circumstances. The good of the "whole" has no meaning to them. These leaders indicated that nothing they did satisfied these individuals, and as one business leader told us, "one or two percent of my employees can eat up 98–99% of my time." Some "high maintenance individuals" were outright nasty and demanding and were never satisfied no matter what accommodations were permitted them. Often, they are talented individuals who potentially could be a real asset to the company. Much like athletic coaches talking about the "upside" of their high maintenance prima donnas, these leaders framed their discussions lamenting how much these talented employees could add if they focused more on their performance and the needs of the company. But they don't; thus, the effort they require is enormous.

Recent research has emerged describing "bullying" in the workplace. *The Monitor on Psychology*, the American Psychological Association's (APA) journal, recently devoted an issue to "office bullies."[5] The cover posed two questions concerning office bullies: "What fosters them?" and "What stops them?" Interestingly, all four stories implied that bullying is common workplace behavior and it goes undetected or worse is permitted. These authors agree that bullying can have significant harmful effects on employees. "Researchers agree," one story wrote, "that bullying is harmful to the health and well-being of victims, organizations and society, likening it to sexual or racial harassment."[6]

What intrigues us about this new interest in workplace bullying is that it is portrayed as emanating from managers or executives down to workers. It is depicted as a top-down phenomenon. However, the information we gleaned concerning difficult employees who affect leaders suggest that bullying may go up as well as down. The APA journal article authors discussed

several definitions of bullying, but according to Helge Hoel, a leading researcher and business psychology professor at the University of Manchester,
"A defining feature of bullying is negative behavior that people feel unable
to defend against or control."[7] We are hesitant to label high maintenance employee behavior as bullying because the definitions are too broad encompassing too many behaviors. But we do believe that this behavior will have negative organization and personal health consequences. And the bullying literature doesn't account for the leadership energy the "extra grace required" takes
to work with such people. It is the "elephant" on the leadership landscape.

One poignant example of the "extra grace" phenomenon was shared by
Jay. He described a faculty member who "had a bi-modal reaction from every person or group with whom he worked." In other words, people either
loved him or hated him. There was never any gray in working with Bradley,
everything was black and white. Jay explained that Bradley was smart, ar-
ticulate, with strong research and teaching skills. In many respects he was a
good faculty member, and in some circumstances, he had a very warm side to
him. "If he would just stop being such a jerk at times," Jay told us, "Bradley
would be a star faculty member." Yet, Bradley was abusive to some people,
had a paranoid streak about people not liking him, and was more demanding than anyone with whom Jay had ever worked. Jay continued explaining
that Bradley's behavior was "on the line of what was acceptable for a university faculty member." Women found him offensive or even abusive; some
students were fearful of him; and many colleagues found him to be terribly
angry, standoffish, and rude. On the other hand, Bradley felt that he was un-
derappreciated, worked harder than anyone else, and wasn't rewarded for his
performance. Jay felt the brunt of Bradley's disdain, and he agonized over the
yearly interactions they had. The pain that Bradley caused is evident as Jay
describes their relationship:

> Nothing in my training or experience prepared me for working with
> Bradley. I tend to think that he is one of a kind, though the university's
> Mediation Officer tells me that his story isn't completely unique. The
> Mediation Officer knows him well as Bradley has filed a grievance over
> his annual performance review every year I've been here. I'm sure he
> did the same to my predecessors. Responding to those grievances is an
> enormous amount of work. One year he actually accused me of age dis-
> crimination, which placed the entire grievance process at another level
> all together. I found that amusing given that I'm five years older than
> Bradley.

But this is not funny at all. I stay up nights thinking about this guy, worrying about potential lawsuits and the incredible amount of my time that he eats up. Many of his colleagues tell me that they are tired of "his act," and they sympathize with my having to deal with him. Every year when he gets angry I get e-mail after e-mail demanding a response. Many e-mails are several pages, single-spaced, in the smallest typeface known to man. When we do his annual performance evaluation each year, there is no rating that satisfies him except for a perfect score. We do this by committee, and the members are so disgusted with how he treats the process that they tend to score him much higher than he deserves to avoid his wrath. He exceeds the page limits we set for the personal reflection portion of the review, and rates himself higher than anyone in the department. He infuriates everyone.

I get to meet with him one-on-one to discuss his evaluation, and those times that he shows up for the meetings are never very pleasant. One time he even showed up with an attorney. He vents all his anger and frustration at me. Another time I asked him to leave my office because he was using inappropriate language concerning his female colleagues. He claimed, inaccurately, that these women were given consideration that wasn't afforded him. He didn't spare the expletives making his outrageous claims.

In our meetings, he demands specific reasons for every word in his performance review and wants to know why he wasn't rated perfectly in every category. No response satisfies him. Interestingly, when some students complained to me about the lack of specificity they received from him for grades they were given, he cried "academic freedom" as his defense when I suggested that he offer the students an explanation.

Time and time again he has caused problems with students and other faculty members, and it is always someone else's fault. Then he files a grievance and threatens lawsuits. It is unnerving and incredibly painful. I took out personal liability insurance to protect myself. My wife worries that he might become violent someday and thinks I should be cautious about meeting with him. It is like nothing I've ever experienced in my life.

Interestingly, another Dean shared a story similar to Jay's tale. Dr. Cuthbert had a faculty member nationally known for his research who challenged his annual performance assessment every year. This faculty member wrote books and consulted all over the country, but he was hardly around to do the grunt work that his department required. He wasn't active in departmental service activities, like working on committees, advising students, being involved in program revision discussions, or preparing accreditation review documents. He just didn't do his share of the work to get the department's basic functions completed. This resulted in his faculty colleagues picking up his slack by serving on extra committees and covering for him when he was away. They resented his behavior, though he just figured it was professional jealousy since he had a national reputation and received large consulting contracts and they did not. Dr. Cuthbert reviewed everyone's annual performance portfolio and based on the expectations for faculty service, he lowered this faculty member's service evaluation as part of the annual performance review. The faculty member went ballistic. He demanded an immediate meeting to see Dr. Cuthbert and screamed at him. Over time, this became a predictable and yearly event. As Dr. Cuthbert explained:

> I hate this part of my work. Every year I can anticipate this loud and nasty response to me doing my job. No objective reviewer would do anything differently. I even sent his file out for review by some peers, and they came to the same conclusion. Each year I review and review his file, prepare well in advance for our annual confrontation, and try my best to provide a sound rationale for the decision. Yet in the weeks and days before we will meet I find myself waking up in the middle of the night thinking about ways I can put this so he'll just understand. But it makes no difference. He's God, and I'm just a mere parishioner in his church. It tends to get ugly and I feel like garbage for days later. The whole thing makes me nervous just thinking about it, and I'm starting to despise the entire annual performance review process just because of this one guy.

One last story came from a businessman who had an employee who was very productive but a pain to work with. Frank had been the division leader for a few years, and most everyone thought he was lucky to have Sam in his area. Sam had what Frank described as a "dual personality." He was good looking, charming, and charismatic, and most everyone who met him liked him. He was very good at what he did. Frank told us that he liked Sam a great deal when he first met him at a national meeting several years ago. But being his boss was a different story. Sam was nasty to every staff person on the job, acted as if everyone worked for him, and challenged everything Frank said. Frank didn't know how to deal with him. Sam was a high producer, but Frank wondered if he was really a benefit to the company. Frank admitted that he didn't have a very thick skin, that he wanted people to like him, and having Sam tell him to his face that he hated him and thought that he was inept really hurt. Frank told us that he stayed awake a lot at night pondering what he could do to make their relationship work. But it seemed to him that the harder he tried, the worse it got. And he wasn't certain that the big bosses would accept a recommendation to let Sam go. Frank figured that they were as taken by Sam as everyone else was. It left him in a real quandary, and he felt like a failure for his inability to make the relationship work. Frank describes the situation:

> It drives me crazy. I've started to question myself and my abilities because of Sam. It makes me wonder if I'm a capable leader. Maybe the others are right and I'm to blame? A few friends I confide with have been very reassuring, but that doesn't minimize the pain I feel. I always thought that doing what was right would be enough. It apparently isn't for me.

These stories highlight the difficulty that leaders face in dealing with these "extra grace required" employees who require extra time, care, and effort. The leaders want these relationships to work, they want to "get it right," but having a high maintenance employee can make the job much more difficult.

WORKING WITH FRIENDS

A related situation common in any work setting involves the leader working with a close friend, or when an employee becomes a friend over the course of years working together. We've all heard stories concerning workplace romance and the sage advice not to date or become romantically involved with a workplace colleague. But working with someone who was a friend for years or became a friend over the course of working together can make for a very difficult and challenging climate for the leader, especially if performance issues erupt. Clearly, there are times when having close personal workplace friends can be a burden for a leader.

Several leaders discussed working with close personal friends, which created situations resulting in increased attention and care. Extra grace was required. Friends like to help friends, but in the workplace this can be problematic. Even though numerous leaders did tell us never to hire a friend, it happens. Sometimes, for example, you hire someone you've worked with before because you know the quality of their work. Think of head football coaches hiring all their assistant coaches. Often they are individuals they have coached with in the past. Then, too, friendships evolve over the course of working closely with someone. Many leaders admit that their closest friends are people with whom they work. Such relationships are inevitable, but when one person is a boss, or over the course of time becomes the boss, it can create tension for the leader, especially when that friend turns out to require that extra grace.

One story involved a director of a unit at a university who was hired the same time as a new faculty member, Dr. Paulen, who ultimately reported to him. They had much in common: they both had young children, they were originally from the same part of the country, and they worked in the same discipline. The friendship solidified over several years. They had coffee together a few times a week, and even got their families together for dinner every once in a while. But their relationship soured over a health care issue for one of Dr. Paulen's children. His daughter was very low functioning and required costly inpatient care. The health care plan refused to cover this "pre-existing" condition. Dr. Paulen continued his previous health coverage from his prior position to cover her care, but the term that was permissible was soon to expire. There wasn't much the leader, John, could do to help as health care benefits were beyond his control, but Dr. Paulen still held him responsible. Dr. Paulen requested a leave to move to a state where he could reactivate his previous health coverage, though he ignored all university rules for requesting such a leave. Instead he moved his family to that new state expecting that he would still be employed full-time by the university. Dr. Paulen's idea was to commute to campus once a month, advise and teach at a distance using electronic technology, and do his research and service in the other state. He wanted John, his friend and the director, to agree to the plan, knowing it was something that the university would not find acceptable.

At first, John tried to work with him. He was able to request and get approved a personal leave for Dr. Paulen well after the timeline for such an application. He spent an inordinate amount of time on this and had to be more assertive than was his nature to get it approved. But, he felt that by providing a personal leave Dr. Paulen would have time to find a new job. He permitted Dr. Paulen to teach some classes in a distance format and even advise by e-mail. But student complaints were mounting and rumors started growing concerning the "absent faculty member." The entire unit was dismayed at what was happening, and John, though sympathetic to Dr. Paulen's situation, was perplexed and unhinged by how it unfolded. The faculty all thought that Dr. Paulen was using his friendship with John to "work the system," and they didn't like it. Nor did the higher-level administrators on campus. With his faculty, students, and superiors on edge, John described the whole situation to us:

I was faced with a real dilemma. My old friend had made some decisions due to his family situation. I didn't necessarily agree with his approach, but I was empathetic toward him. Several nights each week I lay awake agonizing about what was the right thing to do. I'm a father. I know how protecting your children must be a priority. I felt bad for his daughter and family, but really felt as if he had held me and the entire faculty hostage to his own poor decision making. He had known about the health care benefits before accepting the job with us. He had years to resolve it. The fact that things didn't work out is terrible, but he really shared in the responsibility for what happened. Of course, Dr. Paulen didn't see it that way. When we first met he briefly described the situation and told me that they (the university) would have to take care of this. I thought nothing of it at the time, other than wondering if Dr. Paulen knew what he was talking about. I wish the country had a national health care plan. But we don't, and it's not my fault.

The other faculty members in the department were outraged by the whole affair. They felt that the department was being burdened covering for Dr. Paulen. Students weren't pleased never seeing their mentor and only having courses taught electronically. Several complained to me, and I discussed this with Dr. Paulen. He promised to work this out and be around more often. That never happened. I discussed the situation with my boss, and we agreed that in a state-funded institution it would be outrageous to be paying a faculty member to live in another state unless he or she came to campus every week. He was concerned about parental complaints. It was a mess I never saw coming, and though I knew that Dr. Paulen was being unreasonable, he was my friend. So I helped him. He had missed the deadlines for a leave, but I got it approved anyway; I had turned my head to his initial absences from campus. But when he proposed a new plan to be away all but a few days each month, I knew he was being selfish and unfair. I was tested when he called and asked me to help him out, playing on our friendship. What a friend he turned out to be, though I'm sure he feels the same way about me.

I am required to provide renewal/nonrenewal letters for untenured faculty by May 1 each year. I chose not to renew his contract. That would give him one more year as a faculty member, after which he would be gone. . . . I thought this was the fairest thing I could do for him, while also letting the faculty and students know that I was looking out for their best interests. This was an incredibly tough decision for me, but the unit had needs which weren't being met, the faculty were looking at me to resolve the situation, and I felt that Dr. Paulen would let this drag on as long as he could to, "get the university back." . . . The whole affair had an emotional toll on me beyond words.

Two other situations highlight the emotional impact friendships cause organizational leaders. The first involves a woman who worked in a service organization and was asked to lead the performance review for the head of one of the organization's units. Ms. Smith was a unit head at equal rank as Dr. Katz, the woman she was reviewing. These reviews were conducted every five years, and they involved a process of examining performance objectives and results and meeting with people inside and outside the unit to gather information regarding the individual's leadership effectiveness. The review's purpose was to provide feedback to the individual and to serve as the basis for a five-year appointment renewal. In this particular case, Ms. Smith was a close personal friend of Dr. Katz, and she questioned if it was appropriate for her to lead the review team. She was assured by upper-level management that this was not a conflict. In addition Ms. Smith didn't expect any problems since Dr. Katz had a good reputation among the organization's unit leaders. The senior Vice President also had assured her, when she questioned if she was the right person to lead the review, that she would do a great job and that this would be an uncomplicated task. Little did she know when she accepted the assignment how wrong he was!

Ms. Smith and Dr. Katz had been friends ever since Dr. Katz had been hired five years earlier. In fact, Ms. Smith had been on the search committee that had recommended Dr. Katz for the position, and their friendship began when she first started her job. They socialized together, loved sharing "war" stories about their work, had lunch together at least once a week, and generally developed a close personal relationship. Dr. Katz wasn't married, and Ms. Smith knew that she devoted inordinate hours to her job. Ms. Smith figured that with her leading the review she could help to identify some ways of assisting Dr. Katz to be even better at her job than she was. The two of them even talked about her leading the review team. Indeed, Dr. Katz was ecstatic when she learned that her friend was the one appointed to this role, and they discussed the review several times after it started, often over a glass of wine at a weekly TGIF event hosted by a local tavern.

Ms. Smith had a team assigned to work with her. They designed a simple Web-based survey to gather information from two groups: unit members and organizational members. Dr. Katz had established a series of goals years earlier, but the unit's direction had changed and the original goals were outdated. When the first survey results came back with responses from other unit leaders across the organization, they were generally positive, though several wondered if Dr. Katz's unit was really doing anything constructive. That surprised Ms. Smith, and she felt that the feedback on goal clarity and performance might be useful to share with her friend to help her as she moved ahead.

It was the second survey results from Dr. Katz's unit staff and the follow-up interviews that were conducted with them that surprised Ms. Smith. The first hint of a problem came from the survey data. Every single response was very negative regarding Dr. Katz's leadership. People indicated that they felt like they worked on "egg shells," and a good number indicated that unless she was fired they would quit. Most were scathing in their criticism of how she treated people. Common comments included: "she's a witch with no sense of what others might be thinking or feeling," "she is completely out of touch with the people who work for her," "she treats everyone who works for her like dirt and has no respect for anyone she deems to be her inferior," and "she's like a Jekyl and Hyde—she can be sweet as apple pie one minute, then nasty and dismissive the next."

When the Team conducted individual interviews with unit staff members, the depth of the disillusionment and unhappiness was more evident. Simply put, people hated Dr. Katz. She was characterized as "vicious," "nasty," "mean," "inappropriate," and other terms we won't put down on paper. Apparently, she had implemented a rule that prohibited staff to have family members' pictures displayed in their offices because she felt this was unprofessional. One staff member told the Team that, "perhaps if she had ever been married or had a family she wouldn't be so stupid about this. But then again, who on God's earth could live with that woman." Others told how they hated coming to work because she criticized people publicly in the most demeaning ways. After witnessing a colleague face Dr. Katz's wrath, one employee confided, "Nobody should be subjected to that kind of behavior. It was mean and uncalled for. The poor woman being lambasted couldn't stop crying for hours after the interaction."

Ms. Smith had not expected anything like this. What she had felt was going to be a relatively easy task turned into a nightmare. Here was one of her best friends who apparently she really didn't know. They had played and laughed together on so many occasions that she couldn't believe that this was the same Dr. Katz. But every time she inquired about the alleged behavior of her friend the reaction was the same. Dr. Katz was a tyrant who had no business being in a leadership position. It was only those who really didn't know her whom she was able to fool. Ms. Smith realized that she had only interacted with Dr. Katz on a social level, and never in the work setting. But those who did work with her despised her. And Ms. Smith had to author a report to the Vice President with a recommendation for another five-year appointment or recommend some other action. Recommending dismissal was a possibility; however, it had never been recommended before. She also knew that if this peer process was to have any organizational legitimacy, she had to recommend that her friend be fired. The Team discussed this at length, yet they voted unanimously for such a recommendation. The thought of doing this made Ms. Smith physically ill. She had a nagging sense for weeks of what she had to do; still she didn't want to do it. She thought about resigning from being the Team Leader, but it was too late for that. What a mess!

Ms. Smith told us that once she began hearing the negative comments about Dr. Katz she had trouble sleeping. Her health was affected as she worried all the time. She was livid with herself for agreeing to take this assignment on and stressed out about writing the report and discussing it with her boss. Here's how she described it to us:

> I was anxious all the time. I hated writing the report and sealing my friend's fate. But I didn't know what else I could do. I got little comfort that I was doing what was right. My team members kept telling me that we had to be honest in the report and recommend her termination. Terminate someone I ate sushi with just the week before! I knew there was no alternative but to do the job properly, but that didn't help me sleep any better or untie the knot I had in my stomach. I avoided seeing Dr. Katz on several occasions, even ducked into an alley behind a building one time when I saw her walking my way. My husband felt bad for me, but he kept telling me that he always thought that Dr. Katz was a little weird.
>
> This has been the most excruciating work-related event of my life. I think it affected me more than when my grandmother passed away. I know that the sleepless nights and sadness I feel eventually will pass, but I think I'm a different person because of this whole affair. When the vice president thanked me for doing such a good job it didn't bring me any pleasure or comfort.

Ms. Smith's story highlights how devastating it can be when a friendship intertwines with work-related responsibilities. It can lead to discomfort for a leader having to discipline or evaluate the friend's performance. How does someone separate friendship from work responsibilities? Given the stories we have heard and our own experiences, we are not convinced it is possible to compartmentalize such relationships.

A somewhat different scenario is exemplified at a university and involves a faculty member, Danno, who has a drinking problem. Sadly, Danno doesn't think that he has a drinking problem, though he has a pattern of work-related mishaps that put his good friend Franklin, his dean, in a very awkward and tension-filled situation.

Danno and Franklin had developed a friendship over the course of years working together. They worked out together at the university gym sometimes at lunch, and talked occasionally about issues for graduate students. Though they didn't socialize together much after work, they considered one another personal and professional friends and colleagues, and they even collaborated on a few research papers over the years. If asked, Franklin would tell anyone that Danno was a good colleague and a great guy.

Indeed, by just about any measure, Danno was a good faculty member. His students generally liked him, he's known as a good teacher and a competent researcher, he cares about his departmental responsibilities, and he works hard for the good of the whole. When an extra course needed to be taught, Danno volunteered. If a colleague needed help with a complex methodological issue while conducting research, Danno assisted. He's friendly, funny, and most everyone would agree a great guy. In fact, he was assigned to an important administrative role in his department working with graduate students. His annual reviews were always very positive about that work. There also had been some rumors that Danno was a little "too friendly" with some female graduate students. There were no complaints and no sexual advances were suggested, but this was something that people occasionally talked about over coffee or by the water cooler. Franklin tried not to pay attention to rumor or innuendo, and he didn't think much about the rumors since nobody had come to him with any sort of complaint. How quickly that changed!

One spring Danno was conducting an off-site workshop for faculty and graduate students. One evening at the workshop there was alcohol and Danno apparently got drunk and made some inappropriate remarks to a female graduate student. The student was shocked and very dismayed. Also, some people started dancing and Danno took off his shirt and paraded around like a fraternity freshman and not a faculty member leading a workshop. When Franklin learned of this, he approached Danno and asked what had happened. Danno didn't exactly deny anything, as he explained that he had no memory at all of making any comments to the female student or dancing partly naked.

Apparently he had blacked out after getting drunk. The student didn't want to press charges, but she was adamant that something should be done. After talking to Danno, Franklin discussed the situation with the Office of Equal Opportunity on campus, and decided to remove him from his supervisory role working with the departmental graduate students. He was admonished to watch his behavior and a letter of reprimand for his actions and statements was placed in his personnel file. The drinking wasn't mentioned. Danno was thankful as he realized that any sort of investigation could conceivably lead to more significant charges. He thanked Franklin again and again for being his friend. He promised that nothing like this would happen again—a promise that did not last very long.

The next semester some students came to see Franklin and complained about inappropriate remarks that Danno had made in class, and indicated that they thought that his breath smelled of alcohol. A few days later, a faculty member pulled Franklin aside and said that she believed that Danno was intoxicated at a meeting, as his words were all slurred, and he smelled like a strange combination of alcohol, mouth wash, bubble gum and aftershave lotion. Franklin got as much information as he could from the students, who were put off by Danno's reference to lingerie when asking a question of some female students, and they were angered by his suggestion that students meet him for advising at a local bar where the waitresses wear skimpy outfits. Franklin again contacted the university Office of Equal Opportunity to get some guidance on his response. He knew that he had to confront Danno, but he wanted to do it properly and also try to help his friend in any way that he could.

Franklin's wife knew that the situation was tearing her husband up inside. She found him awake at night making notes about the situation when he was considering what to do. She suggested that he end the friendship, in her words, "to protect yourself." But Franklin liked Danno, and besides being his boss, he was his friend. He didn't see how abandoning the friendship would help anything. He found himself worrying about the next inappropriate story he would hear about Danno. Ultimately he decided to be proactive and meet with Danno to get his side of the story and to offer some advice. Franklin had been warned that alcoholism is a disease, and it was beyond his authority to mandate treatment, especially if there was no solid proof that alcoholism was there and impacting his job performance. What Franklin came to realize was that Danno's inappropriate behavior was associated with his being drunk. As he poked around he learned that many faculty and students believed that Danno was an alcoholic. Many had stories to share about him. None of this made Franklin's job any easier.

When they got together Franklin brought along the Alcoholic's Anonymous test for identifying alcoholism. In answering the questions Franklin was certain that Danno was an alcoholic. He wanted to share this with his friend to get him to seek help. He told Danno a story that they both knew quite well, about a mutual friend at a state agency who had gotten drunk at a party and fell down some stairs breaking some bones. But he never sought any treatment for his alcoholism and eventually hit some kids with his car on a dark rainy night, and due to his alcohol-blood level he was jailed for manslaughter. Franklin emphasized that he didn't want to ever have to visit his friend in jail, and that Danno's wife and kids needed him around. Danno was again overly thankful, he cried and thanked Franklin for being such a great friend, but he never admitted to being an alcoholic or agreed to any sort of treatment. He left by saying that he would think about everything they discussed. Franklin made a mental note to himself that reminded him that the first sign on the road to recovery was accepting that you had a drinking problem. He was pretty certain that Danno wasn't there yet.

Franklin knew that without treatment the problems wouldn't go away. As he described the situation to us, he said that Danno was putting his job at risk and that he was "an accident waiting to happen." But it was still terribly agonizing for him. Here's how he described it:

I wasn't sure what to do. By telling Danno that he needed help, that I thought he was an alcoholic and even brought along the AA test to prove my point, I probably had violated any number of employment laws and regulations. But I felt I had to do something to help this guy. Though everyone liked him, they felt he was a problem. Several women in the department told me that we shouldn't let him get away with his sexist comments and behavior. They were all looking to me to do something. I was worried for his life and his job, but I just wasn't sure how best to help him. This whole affair kept taking up more and more of my time. I was warned to document everything that I did in case there was litigation. The lawyers told me all the things I could and couldn't do. But I just wanted to help a friend. It literally became an obsession with me as I was fixated on how to resolve this mess. How was I to get this guy to admit that he had a problem? It took me a long time to realize that some "tough love" was about the best I could do for someone that didn't want to help himself. Months later, I'm still waiting for the next bomb to fall about Danno. I've dreamed about getting a phone call from the police informing me that he'd killed someone. It's so sad and so excruciating for me. I just find it hard to let go and stop thinking about it.

All these stories share the common characteristic of leaders being put in very uncomfortable situations due to the involvement of friends. Dealing with friends in the workplace requires extra care. Though these scenarios may have been stressful if anyone was involved, the fact that personal friends were a part of these situations made the events much harder for the leaders to deal with. There certainly are those leaders who are able to move beyond these types of situations fairly easily. For example, one leader involved in such a situation told us, "I lost someone who I thought was a friend, but learned the lesson that you can't put individual friendship above treating the larger whole with the respect they deserve." But for many leaders, dealing with the idiosyncrasies of working with a high maintenance employee or making personnel decisions that involve friends can be agonizing.

CHAPTER 5

Coping with Emotions on the Job

You've got to have a thick skin.

—a small-business owner

Throughout the course of our research we kept hearing how important it is to be able to deal well with people and find ways to avoid overreacting. "You've got to have a thick skin" was something that several leaders emphasized to us in describing how they dealt with difficult personal interactions and the concomitant reactions that were evoked. Scholars studying the workplace know that being skillful in dealing with people and learning how to control emotions increasingly is becoming important. *A Harvard Business Review* article emphasized that point very succinctly:

> The rules of work are changing. We're being judged by a new yardstick: not just by how smart we are, or by our training and expertise, but also by how well we handle ourselves and each other. This yardstick increasingly is being applied in choosing who will be hired and who will not, who will be let go and who retained, who passed over and who promoted.[1]

But how should leaders cope with the many feelings that their work will engender? The answer isn't easy to pinpoint. We have a mutual friend who is a psychologist. His office is a professional-looking place, with comfortable plush chairs and a couch appropriately spaced around hardwood floors and fancy-looking rugs. The office is so warm and inviting that it makes you want to start sharing your innermost feelings. Off in the corner is a funny-looking stuffed creature that looks like it might be a bad replica of the lead movie character of *ET* (*Extra-Terrestrial*). During a visit we both figured that he probably treated kids as part of his practice and needed toys in the office. We frankly thought nothing of it.

Recently we were discussing navigating workplace emotions with a fairly renowned psychologist, who after listening to our ideas, pulled out the same funny-looking creature from a closet and pushed on its foot. In a vaguely seductive but soft-sounding deep female voice, our ET-like friend said, "Everything will be all right." In shock, we gazed over at the good professor, who smiled and explained, "It's my Therapy Buddy." We came to learn that the Therapy Buddy has become popular with psychologists and others in almost a cult-like way. Google "Therapy Buddy" and you'll turn up more sites than you could imagine. We learned that there are Therapy Buddy T-shirts, which the inventor made to help him with his fear of flying; that a fellow tried to bring his Therapy Buddy with him to the Emmy Award show to interview the stars; and that it has appeared on the ABC TV show *American Inventor*. For about $70 you can get a Therapy Buddy, what one site described as a psychologist's tool. Another site explained:

> My Therapy Buddy is a transitional object. It's a wonderfully soft and huggable friend. My Therapy Buddy for psychotherapy, trauma, anxiety, depression, psychic, emotional or transitional therapy. A teddy bear like therapeutic companion for distress, counseling and therapy.[2]

We're not psychologists, and with deference to the manufacturers of the toy and those who use their "Buddies" for therapeutic purposes, we remain skeptical about providing Therapy Buddies to managers and leaders as a means for effectively eradicating the emotional effects they deal with at work. Instead we have learned that coping is difficult and requires some planning and reflection. Through the stories we heard we found that leaders have ways for dealing with emotions that attach to decisions that they make. In this chapter we will share coping mechanisms leaders have developed to deal with their work's emotional side. In the next chapter we will set out strategies for planning for the emotional situations that leaders will inevitably confront.

There are numerous ways that people deal with emotional issues they face. This is true for leaders as well. Some positive approaches we heard related to personal physical and mental heath. Leaders told us they exercised, took walks, found time to think and reflect, and relied on friends and colleagues for support. We consider these activities to be healthy reactions to stress and all are discussed in books and research papers examining job-related stress.[3] Of course, there are unhealthy reactions as well. Other leaders jokingly described drinking away their emotional stress at "the corner bar." We sensed that for some leaders this was more than a simple joke, and perhaps reflected serious mental or physical problems that resulted from emotional stress. Still others described taking their stress and anxiety home with them, or occasionally acting out with other organizational members due to the pressure they were feeling. Research on office bullying has shown that middle-level managers bullied by senior executives often take out their frustrations by bullying those who work for them.[4] This cycle of emotional stress and emotional reaction isn't healthy for the individuals involved or the organization they serve and has significant negative consequences.

We analyzed the stories we heard and three coping strategies leaders found successful emerged. Coping is a reaction to stimuli. At the same time, emotional reactions to workplace interactions are predictable. Thus, though the strategies we develop are not preventive and do not eliminate emotional reactions or even assist preventing them, they were means leaders used to deal with the emerging emotions. Perhaps these strategies helped them find meaning from very difficult and uncomfortable situations. These coping strategies helped the leaders to move ahead when their gut reaction ordinarily may have held them back.

There is an expansive literature on coping with stress and burnout. We make no attempt in this chapter to address all the varied strategies available for those seeking coping mechanisms for the emotional stress they'll face in the workplace. We note, for example, the rapid growth in popularity of what is referred to as positive psychology, or the psychology of hope. Within that field there is an emphasis on optimism and various techniques offered for identifying individual strengths and reacting more positively to life's experiences.[5] Anyone interested in learning how to deal with emotional dissonance will certainly benefit from an understanding of this growing field of interest in the world of psychology. Therapy in this psychological paradigm also focuses on prevention strategies.

But in analyzing our data, we focused on what the leaders we interacted with identified as their coping mechanisms. The three coping strategies we discovered were: (1) *Finding Order Out of Chaos*; (2) *Communicating and Strategizing as Keys*; and (3) *Following Your Heart*. In each instance, the leaders shared ways they made sense out of the difficult emotional situations they confronted that ultimately helped them address what otherwise could have been a more debilitating outcome. The leaders tried to find the proverbial "silver lining" in the most emotional circumstances. These leaders wanted to be constructive and proactive when they were in stressful situations, and they tried to feel that they made the right decision.

FINDING ORDER OUT OF CHAOS

Leaders expressed that there were positives that could be drawn even during the most emotionally laden situations. Our interpretation draws from research on complex adaptive systems that have been evolving in the hard sciences and more recently in economics and other social sciences.[6] As discussed in Chapter 2, the most telling work has come out of the Santa Fe Institute, where researchers who studied quantum physics found that the linear and predictable models explaining how systems work are wrong. In open systems, whether in the quantum world or living organisms, the world is far more complex than originally thought. The very mechanistic worldview has dominated Western culture since Newton's little apple landed on his head, and scientists developed theories that treated all aspects of our lives as being much like a machine. But, as Sir Karl Popper put it, an early proponent criticizing the mechanical visions of the scientific community, the world operates more like clouds than a clock. Life is fuzzy, irrational, nonlinear, and certainly not predictable. Franz Capra described this push toward determinism this way:

> Like human-made machines, the cosmic machine was thought to consist of elementary parts. Consequently, it was believed that complex phenomena could always be understood by reducing them to their basic building blocks and by looking for mechanisms through which these interacted. This attitude, known as reductionism, has become so deeply ingrained in our culture that it has often been identified with the scientific method. The other sciences accepted the mechanistic and reductionistic views of the classical physics as the correct description of reality and molded their own theories accordingly. Whenever psychologists, sociologists, or economists wanted to be scientific, they naturally turned toward the basic concepts of Newtonian physics.[7]

The problem, as we learned from the more recent complex systems research, is that the universal principles we relied on aren't universal at all. Instead, what we now know is that in human organizations, much like with cells or organs, large numbers of agents (individuals in human settings) interact with one another in many ways. Human systems find order through these individual interactions through a process called emergence. In other words, the whole is greater than the parts or their sums. Thus, through working together we end up with a greater purpose achieved through the whole than could ever have been realized individually. Such systems also are constantly adapting to their environment, and are always in a dynamic state. Open systems constantly are reorganizing to meet their environmental needs. Ilya Prigogine's Nobel Award-winning research in chemistry referred to these as dissipative systems, because a system's energy loss (entropy) doesn't lead necessarily to its demise, but instead it releases present forms so new structures emerge, better suited to the current environment.[8]

This is complicated research, but just consider that over time the Berlin Wall fell, the Soviet Union split apart, the European Union was conceived, and any array of unpredictable outcomes we could cite evolved where old systems gave way to new structures. Margaret Wheatley's *Leadership and the New Science* suggested that the ramifications of the new research in the sciences are significant for those leading organizations:

> I no longer believe that organizations can be changed by imposing a model developed elsewhere. So little transfers to, or even inspires, those trying to work at change in their own organization . . . and much more important, the new physics cogently explains that there is no objective reality out there waiting to reveal its secrets. There are no recipes or formulae, no checklists or advice that describe "reality." There is only what we create through our engagement with others and with events. Nothing really transfers; everything is always new and different and unique to each of us.[9]

For our research purposes this sense that systems find order out of chaos was a powerful metaphor for these leaders' stories. Complex adaptive systems, though constantly in a state of disequilibrium, find order through their interactions as a result of spontaneous self-organization. The leaders were clear that something emerged for them as a result of the organizational distress they experienced. Through their chaotic emotional experience they were able to create knowledge that would serve them well the next time they were challenged emotionally at work. It helped them cope with what could have been an even more stressful experience.

The most common reaction that falls under this theme "Order Out of Chaos" was the learning that took place among the leaders with whom we spoke. Many discussed what they learned and how they evolved due to their emotional experiences. Similarly, but less often, the leaders discussed how the experience forced them to reassess their values, which was also a learning experience. Jeannie was a community college president on a small campus in a mid-Western state. Her faculty called her Dr. J. She was well liked on campus and respected across her community. Her weekly informal gatherings with faculty and staff were well attended. But when her school experienced a crisis, she quickly learned that the collegial support she took for granted wasn't as solid as she had imagined. The situation she faced is something every leader fears—an incident at work that led to several deaths. It is a crisis that nobody ever wants to confront. The police get involved, people need time to heal, and work comes to a complete halt. Unfairly, some people blamed her for the incident and felt she bore some responsibility for the deaths. They felt that she could have had more preventive measures in place. Even some friends were vocal in their anger. In our conversation, she wondered what caused their distrust. "One minute I'm having coffee and sharing a donut with someone," she said, "and the next minute I'm the devil incarnate."

Jeannie was shocked by this reaction and it hurt. "What did they expect me to do," she told us, "have a crystal ball and predict the future? Is that what they think leaders are supposed to do?" The police were great. They made her realize that incidents involving shootings and job-related accidents are unpredictable. Along the way, she came to appreciate that many incidents are unexpected, and there was nothing she could have done to change what happened. Jeannie explained, "It's so easy to be an armchair quarterback and take your anger out on the person in charge. I came to realize that it wasn't really them talking, but the anger and fear that gripped our whole community. Who else could they have lashed out at but me?" Obviously, she was able to turn this very emotional situation into a learning experience. And she was certain that having gone through it, as difficult as it was, would serve her well in the future.

A school district leader we met had a similar epiphany. His situation didn't involve a death, but involved a campus situation that brought out the best and worst from people in his school. It was dismaying to him initially, but he was able to step back and draw some cogent ideas to help him as he evolved as a leader. Note the very thoughtful self-analysis that he shared with us:

> Things I learned included that no location can be isolated from this type of incident. Procedures must be in place, even on rural campuses. Everyone must be prepared. Also, take into account the human factor. There are many ways that people respond to things, including family dynamics. Finally, never underestimate the length of time and the intensity of the reverberations. The past comes alive, situations come to the fore, and things are triggered. There is connectiveness of the human race: people respond to what happens to someone else and the personal agony

relating to it. And put aside expectations for the way people relate. It can be very surprising, but however it manifests itself, it must be taken seriously.

Individuals with whom you work are unpredictable; they may react to differing stimuli in unknown ways as is apparent in this leader's self-reflection. Though this superintendent calls for rules and procedures to cover possible incidents that may never occur, it is clear that he will never downplay what he might consider as silly interactions or issues if people raise them as concerns.

In our conversations we spoke with leaders taking their organizations through a change process. Sometimes this included layoffs and other cutbacks; other times it meant switching job responsibilities or roles for workers. It never was easy and without hardships. We've already shared stories of how agonizing such situations can be for the one who must carry out the personnel changes. But we also found leaders who were inspired by what they learned. It proved to be a powerful coping mechanism. Not only did these leaders feel that they were making the correct decision, they also grew in their ability to lead their organizations. One businessman described a very emotional experience he had with putting through a structural change that included firing and moving people around. Several had their responsibilities downgraded. But somehow he grew from this. He identified several strategies to employ if ever he had to go through this again:

At each level, I learned and I grew and I benefited. One of the lessons that I share with people all the time is that as a leader, don't be afraid to learn. Because you constantly will be faced with obstacles or situations that you have not faced before. You've got to deal with those. You are going to be facing people who don't believe in you, don't trust you, or for whatever reason are trying to tear you down. As long as you know you're making the best decisions you can make with the information you have and you're doing the best you can, you just keep doing it. Bring people together. Work with people because you are there because they put you there.

These same themes echoed through the stories we collected and conversations we held. Perhaps the most detailed explanation came from a superintendent who had gone through what he described as the most emotionally draining experience in his life. "Nothing," he told us, "had prepared me for this feeling. I felt betrayed, worn out, and even questioned my very job choice. I know that my wife and family were worried about me, and I found myself worrying about me as well." But somehow he was able to reframe this incredibly hard experience into something positive. He found order out of chaos. He reached a point where he could step back, reframe what he had experienced, and grew from even the most devastating experience of his life.

> Although I learned many lessons from that experience, five have affected the way I live my life to this day. First, I cannot replenish myself by myself. For me there has to be a higher power. Second, I learned that in leadership you sometimes have to suffer in the short run to bring people along with you for the whole journey. Third, I learned that being polite, courteous, compassionate and caring no matter what is said to me or about me in return costs nothing. My own self-respect remains intact and that is worth everything. Fourth, I learned that underneath peoples' ugliness, hostility, and nasty behavior there is fear. Fear of losing a job, fear of being rejected. Fear can take on so many disguises that I have learned to always look for that first in a really contentious situation. Fifth, I have finally learned that when we talk about ethics we are talking not about "right" and "wrong," but "right" and "right." And there is no right way to do the wrong thing.

This self-reflection that resulted from an emotionally draining experience was especially evident in several leaders' stories we heard from those who learned how to respond to various stimuli. Research on conflict identifies several possible reactions to conflict situations, and the proper response is dictated by the specifics inherent in each experience. So just reacting with a gut response will work in some situations, but not others.[10] For example, if everyone is pretty hot under the collar, then avoidance may be an appropriate response. More than likely some collaborative approach is the best possible scenario as it leads to a "win/win" experience for all involved. But concerning the emotional situations and reactions that our leaders discussed, we found it heartening to hear that many leaders took stock of their own emotions and how they reacted to them. For example, a school administrator provided a very succinct description of this very significant reflection. As an aside, since principals deal with kids, teachers, and parents on a daily nonstop train ride for nine months a year, having personal reflections seems particularly important for them. But likely such thinking would help any leader. Here is what our principal had to say about what he took from a very intense emotional experience with which he dealt:

So, what have I learned? That it's very important as an administrator to understand what situations might potentially "push our buttons." These buttons are very ingrained in us because of past experiences, our personalities, and our value systems. I've realized that I actually like to fight—indeed, I am a fighter and a survivor. But when I don't keep that trait in check when carrying out administrative tasks and responsibilities, I do not serve myself well.

In a few instances, these leaders revealed how they learned from their direct confrontations. As we discussed in Chapter 4, those are generally the most difficult leadership interactions, especially if a friend is involved. If you are trying to help someone grow and improve, and he or she chooses to ignore your efforts, it can be demoralizing and stressful. But as Steve explained to us, he learned the hard way that being upfront and helpful may not have any effect. In his business people had to constantly learn new techniques or they quickly became outdated. He pulled aside many employees and offered them the assistance they would need to succeed. But many just ignored him. It was hard to take, as he knew that they were ultimately, in his own words, "digging their own graves." But they chose not to accept his advice. And despite the emotional strain this put on him, his relationship with his workers, and their longevity with the company (and the ultimate time he would have to hand them their layoff papers), he was able to take something positive from the mess that ensued. As he put it,

> Probably the greatest lesson I learned was that you can be straightforward, as helpful as providing lots of assistance to the person, but unless the person knows and comes to accept the fact that he needs to change, they won't . . . you have to learn those things the hard way.

Like the psychotherapist who can't change behavior unless the patient wants help, Steve learned that even his best efforts to help someone succeed were for naught when those he was trying to help didn't respond. This isn't easy for a leader to accept, but it is something that Steve had to accept.

Dr. Gaines had a similar experience though his situation involved a dear friend with whom he had worked for over five years. His friend chose to ignore his advice and counsel, wouldn't change or expand his skills, and ultimately had to be let go. When the ax fell, his friend was livid with him for "not protecting him," but eventually Dr. Gaines came to accept that he had gone out of his way to be kind and helpful. It just didn't work, though for weeks the entire situation had been a drain on him emotionally. But along the way,

Dr. Gaines tried to convince his friend that he had to change, yet each attempt was politely, but consistently, ignored. His friend kept saying, "we've been in this business a long time, these things come and go, don't worry, things will be fine." But "things" weren't fine, and Dr. Gaines knew it. Others in the company were starting to get weary of the supposed "slack" that this friend was getting, though Dr. Gaines assured us that he would have done the same for anyone. Ultimately, when he was feeling at a low point during the crisis, Dr. Gaines took stock of what he had experienced and drew a strong lesson. As he put it:

> I lost someone whom I thought was a friend, but learned the lesson that you can't put individual friendship above treating the larger whole with the respect they deserve.

Clearly, these leaders were a resilient group who grew from their emotional experiences. They were self-referent in examining what had transpired and drew upon their lessons to improve their leadership. Ultimately, the growth that took place for the leaders was the basis for their being able to move beyond a devastating experience. They adapted and learned finding order from the emotional chaos.

COMMUNICATING AND STRATEGIZING AS KEYS

As the leaders became increasingly aware of their emotional burden, they came to believe that it was imperative to be as open with their employees as possible. They discussed the need for communicating with everyone to keep them informed and to help them work through the issues being confronted. As one leader explained to us, "there was absolutely no reason at all that I had to keep this bottled up inside of me." Another told us, "I just found it helped everyone to talk through the issues."

One common thread was that open communication was healthy for all company employees including the leader. It was seen as an ethical imperative to be open and honest, and it provided leaders an opportunity to talk through and think through the issues causing concern. Many saw this as very self-protective; their own position could be compromised by an event and the behaviors that resulted, so sharing information was seen as crucial to everyone's understanding what the decisions were and why they were being made. Of course, at times there were privacy issues (e.g., dismissal of an employee), which inhibited the ability to talk too much about what was happening. But there was a common belief among the leaders that sharing information was a way to help them get through even the most difficult situations.

One example came at a community college where restructuring and retrenchment were being implemented. The news had been rumored for months. Everyone was tense. The president had worked at another institution when she was a faculty member and had undergone a similar scenario. She recalled how unsettling it had been on everyone when it seemed that nobody knew for certain exactly what was happening. In fact, Laura had written her doctoral dissertation on retrenchments in a time of what was popularly called reengineering in business. She had prepared case studies of several corporations that went through it. So, while she was aware of how she might handle the situation, she had never been the person having to implement such changes. The whole situation was bad enough, but the fact that it was unfolding just before Christmas was unfortunate. It was very hard on her, but she persevered. Here is how she explained how she handled it:

> Knowing how quickly bad news spreads, I inserted this issue into the agenda for my scheduled faculty meeting at the end of the week. This gave me time to update the president's cabinet on Wednesday and the Faculty Senate on Thursday before the Friday faculty meeting. I knew ahead of time that the gallows humor would be rampant about an early Christmas present and Scrooge and the rest that goes with an end of fall term negative announcement. But I also realized that what I had to say about the overstaffing issue, the information I had gathered, and faculty involvement would be more positive than the gloom and doom the grapevine would spew forth.

A business leader had similar advice regarding the importance of sharing information. While his company wasn't contemplating a complete shutdown, sales and profits were down and attention to the bottom line by those leading the company was paramount. Josh knew he had to make some changes and felt that the best way to stave off a complete collapse of morale was to get everyone involved. "Giving them a stake in the process," he told us, was the right way to move ahead when times were tough. It also provided him a way to seek ideas about what to do and to avoid the sense of being all by himself on a deserted island. He was very clear about all the positives that open communication can bring to a company even in the worst situations:

> I believe in inclusion, in the importance of all to the whole, in the importance of the process of creation. In November, I sent out communications focusing on the importance of recruiting and cautioning against unnecessary spending . . . I met with groups and individuals, sent out memos

and e-mails, and solicited input, ideas and feedback. The open communication elicited great suggestions.

An interesting issue related to open communications was mentioned by those in public settings. In public institutions, or in private companies that have a big stake in a local community, the media can become an important means to share information. While the media have their own rules, several leaders described how they used the media to help them through difficult situations. "You can't hide anything from them," one leader explained, "as they'll spin things any way they want to. Since you can't really control the media, you are better off working with them. It is almost a form of cooptation for me." Note this very clear message a college president sends:

> How to handle the media becomes critical in traumatic situations because you can be sure that the media will be there. You must be fast, and you must be the initiator or it puts you in a vulnerable situation...it is also essential for any community relations people to do a good job...informing students about college resources is critical. There are services available in any kind of crisis situation, any kind of jeopardy, for any kind of problem.

The leaders regarded open communication as essential for dealing with the emotional issues they faced. Open communication helped the leaders survive a difficult time and protected them as they worked with their colleagues. It was a common coping strategy that they employed. For many it was simply the right action to take, and it made them feel a little bit better when finding any solace was difficult. Several leaders explained that sharing as much information as possible made the decisions feel as if they were shared by everyone, and in a sense "de-isolated" those in charge. As many leaders explained, open communication provided damage control for both the betterment of the organization and for their own mental health.

FOLLOWING YOUR HEART

The final strategy the leaders employed in coping was their feeling that they were doing the right thing. There is no doubt these leaders were faced with making very difficult decisions, and these decisions had emotional implications for them. But it was uncanny how many leaders were clear that they had taken the right action. Although this didn't overcome the pain they experienced in working through the issues they faced, it helped. In our minds, this was an obvious way these leaders coped with decisions that impacted their lives and those with whom they worked. Making the decisions was never easy, but once they were made, they didn't look back. They still may be upset over aspects of what happened, but at some point they let go of self-blame. Instead, many leaders believed that their action was consistent with the organization's collective good. In "following their hearts," these leaders expressed confidence that they were performing for the collective good.

One leader was clear that he had followed his heart. This dean had to deal with a close friend, and we've already discussed how emotionally unsettling that can be. But he made the decision to dismiss his friend and had to live with the feelings of hurting someone about whom he cared so much. But at the same time, he believed he had made the correct decision. He expressed this very succinctly:

> The whole affair was very hurtful, as I felt I was overly supportive of someone who didn't treat me with equal respect. I left the situation quite dismayed, but with a strong sense that I had done what was right for the College. The faculty were very supportive of me and angry at the way Dr. Xavier had dealt with them. . . . In the end, I gathered a good deal of strength in the knowledge that I was doing what was right, and although it was okay to lend a colleague some help, the ultimate decision had to be related to the collective good.

Another college leader had made some very draconian budget cuts that impacted many faculty and staff. Some were dismissed, others moved into different departments. Salaries had to be frozen for several years, and while most cuts were done through attrition, it wasn't always possible. Travel monies were frozen, staff let go, and it wasn't even clear if all the cuts would save the school. The president was hopeful about the future, she knew the cuts had to be made, but the whole affair was hard. This president used an open process so that communication was apparent, but she worried for her future since such a situation could end her career as a leader, whether with this school or any other. Nobody, she explained, ever wants to be associated with making budget cuts, and she was concerned if anyone in the school would ever say anything nice about her. But interestingly, she found some relief knowing that she was doing the right thing. It was a way she coped with what was a terribly emotionally experience for her:

> I do not know the long-term impact this will have. I have worked hard to be open, fair, forthcoming. I have acted in good faith. I have tried to

be inclusive, to take advantage of the talent and knowledge across the institution. Yet, I accept responsibility for all the decisions that have been made . . . my hopes for the future and my dreams for the college—for my college—are increasingly clear. I still have the passion . . .

One final story exemplifies how leaders coped by feeling that they had done the right thing by following their heart. A small college president told us the story of coming to a new campus that was facing some very difficult issues. He presented the information to the faculty, and put them to work on a number of projects aimed at saving as many jobs and programs as possible. There was resentment. Apparently his predecessors had allowed some issues to fester and never did anything to protect the school from the fallout that would inevitably follow. The situation was worse since the prior administration had been in place for years and the leaders were widely loved and respected. But the new president knew full well that they had been very self-serving and had refused to make the kinds of decisions necessary to protect the school's future. The entire mess was left to the new guy and his team, and he resented it. When he first realized how bad the situation was, he had started taking long walks to talk to himself. He questioned his decision to take this presidency, feeling that it had been his urge to move into a top position that had clouded his thinking and avoid finding out what was really happening. He knew that the projects he had implemented would be very stressful, and some people would be hurt by the outcomes. But he eventually found some relief in grasping that doing what he had set in place was the right thing.

> As I was wont to do in those days I took a long weekend alone and went to the ocean. I wanted to reconnect with my soul. It didn't take long to realize how incredibly saddened I was by what we were doing and by what was going to have to take place. I felt angry and resentful that previous leaders had dropped the ball and had let the faculty down. That they didn't have the courage it took to make tough decisions along the way. On and on this righteous indignation went until I remembered those walks to campus last summer when I, too, was praying for a miracle. Anything, Lord, that would save me from having to make tough decisions. Suddenly, I was filled with a compassion I had not felt before. I realized that those projects were their man-made miracles . . . that I was on the right path.

These leaders' made some difficult decisions. Yet, in the end, they felt they had done what was correct and gained a sense of contentment by following their heart. One way to cope was to feel that they were acting in the best interest of the organization. The leaders were true to their heart and carried out decisions that felt right. As one businessman told us, "I have to look at myself in the mirror each morning. I'm not the coldhearted son of a gun that many may think of me. When I like what I see in that mirror, I know that I've done what was right."

Leaders make difficult decisions all the time. Many of these decisions can be very emotional for the boss. The leaders we worked with had several strategies for coping with the emotional life they led. They tried to find positives out of the emotional murkiness they went through, usually some learning that would serve them well in the future. They learned that being honest and open in communicating with their employees brought them some satisfaction implementing decisions that could have negative consequences for a lot of people. And finally, they did what they thought was right; they followed their hearts. Anyone in a leadership role will need strategies for coping with the emotions that will undoubtedly arise. Ignoring these will likely hurt personally, and probably affect how well the organization thrives.

But coping while on the job after making decisions is much like trying to implement changes in a plane's design while the plane is in flight. It is a lot easier to try to prepare for emotional issues before they actually emerge. In other words, along with coping strategies that will be used while the plane is in flight, leaders should have a plan for dealing with emotions before the plane takes off. It is this kind of emotional blueprint we turn to in the next chapter.

CHAPTER 6

Planning for an Emotional Future

I can't go through anything like this again. I've got to figure out a better way to deal with these gut-wrenching situations.

—university administrator

Emotions are ubiquitous, in the home, at work, and throughout the course of our lives. Humans are emotional beings. Yet emotions have been largely ignored in work-related training and preparation programs. David Caruso and Peter Salovey describe the situation this way:

> *Emotions are important.* They are relevant to our everyday lives. They are not merely vestiges of our evolutionary past, like our wisdom teeth or appendix. Nonetheless, for all the importance of emotions, they receive so little attention in our formal education that we are woefully inadequate when it comes to understanding and dealing with them.[1]

At the same time, though interest in the concept of emotional intelligence is beginning to change this emphasis, most businesses and organizations have relegated any understanding of human emotions to the periphery of what is important for success. This is especially true for those aspiring to leadership positions. In a world with its eye sharply focused on grasping the brass ring, emotions fall outside what most of us even think about in preparing for our success. The reason is probably best explained by two European scholars, who noted that, "it is almost commonplace to observe that organizational emphases on rationality have led to the relative neglect of emotional issues in organizational life."[2] But as we've emphasized in the preceding chapters, emotions play an important role in the real world of leadership. Sometimes helpful, often agonizing, it is clear that every leader will face an emotionally laden future.

We don't pretend to be organizational psychologists with the ability to suggest all the ways that emotions can impact your work life. We certainly don't have the TV astrologers' skills who offer insights into how the future will unfold so you might plan your life accordingly. But we've both been in leadership positions when emotions bubbled up and took hold of us. We know how emotions can knot you up during "business as usual." One leader described the feeling attached to such times as the equivalent of being hit with a sucker punch right in the solar plexus. Another described these emotions as overwhelming her entire existence, sitting on the forefront of her mind every waking moment like a stalled car in heavy traffic.

Thankfully, our research has taught us how leaders can plan for the cornucopia of emotions they will confront as part of their work. We see such planning as an indispensable skill any leader can employ to be successful. Nobody can plan for all the situations and contingencies they will confront. If only life were so predictable! But once you accept that you will face an array of situations that will have an emotional impact, you can begin to ready yourself for this inevitable future. Remember that emotions impact your interactions with others and even your ability to do your job. Simply put, they affect your performance. So being prepared for what you will ultimately face is a worthwhile strategy to have. One of the many tools you'll need to survive and even excel as the leader in charge.

To offer a recommendation for some thoughtful planning is certainly not a revolutionary notion. Success in any domain requires a level of planning. A study that Ginsberg did on adults with learning disabilities who were highly successful in their careers found that such individuals exerted an unusual amount of control to foster their success. There were a series of internal decisions that had to be made, and some external manifestations all labeled as adaptability that fostered the control they needed to succeed. The research team described the issue of control this way:

> Control refers to the drive to manage one's life. This control involved a set of internal decisions (conscious decisions to take charge of one's life) and external manifestations (adapting and shaping oneself to move ahead). Attaining control is the key element for success. Adults with learning disabilities work throughout their lives to learn how to take control of their existence. It undergirds their ultimate success.[3]

What became evident was that taking control involved a high degree of thought and planning. Though the specific requirements may differ for those who have learning disabilities, the key role for planning in achieving success was obvious.

Planning is crucial for success in any business or professional setting. A notable example is in the world of information technology, where organizations are constantly working to plan ways to offer protection for their technology systems. Much like the leader dealing with the fallout of decisions that may affect his or her emotions, this is a high-stakes field where the slightest breach of security can have enormous financial and personal implications when information is compromised. True "techies" know that every technology system is highly vulnerable. We've all read the headlines about situations where a technology system was compromised and the vital personal information of thousands of people was exposed. To cope with this uncertainty and constant security threat facing organizations, programs have been developed to assist with the planning necessary to protect the vital information stored in any computer or Web-based system. The Software Engineering Institute at Carnegie Mellon University, for example, developed OCTAVE—Operationally Critical Threat, Asset, and Vulnerability Evaluation.[4] OCTAVE is described as a risk-based strategic assessment and planning technique for security. It involves the appointment of an Analysis Team that leads the organization through three phases of workshops and investigations that:

- Identify critical assets and the threats to those assets.
- Identify the vulnerabilities that expose those threats.
- Develop an appropriate protection strategy for the organization's mission and priorities.

Planning in the high-risk world of information security is obviously a key for success for every organization. Breaches are costly and can undermine the work the organization is striving to achieve. The planning won't necessarily diffuse all security breaches, but it is a means for coping with the inevitable security concerns that every technology system confronts. We conclude that planning for the emotion-laden world of leadership is similarly important. Such planning won't short-circuit emotional reactions to decisions that are made, but it can help you deal with those emotions as they find their way into your psyche.

So how do you plan for the emotions you'll face in the corner office? During the course of our research we've discovered a number of interrelated ideas that have emerged and provide useful frameworks and processes for leaders wishing to prepare themselves for the inevitable onslaught of emotions they will encounter. In the next few pages we'll review ideas about emotional regulation, emotional competence, emotional awareness, and the emotional blueprint that other researchers have analyzed and presented as means for planning for the emotions associated with work. We'll also provide a set of lessons derived from our analysis of these concepts and strategies integrated with the themes from the data we collected. There clearly is an emerging literature on dealing with workplace-related emotions. Our goal is to present the best thinking on the subject informed by the ideas cultivated from the leaders we studied.

One caveat must be appreciated. There is no simple panacea as not all work settings are the same. The literature on leadership has demonstrated the situational and contingent nature of leading an organization, how different approaches work best in differing situations. It also is true that certain types of work will be prone to emotional interactions. Some research, for example, highlights the centrality of emotions in hospitality and service organizations where a high degree of customer satisfaction is important.[5] Our point is that while developing abilities to deal with emotions is important for any leader, since leadership entails direct involvement with people in guiding the work of the organization, we recommend emotional planning while recognizing that the needs and skills necessary in differing settings with different people will be quite variable.

EMOTIONAL REGULATION

Learning to regulate one's emotions would be an invaluable skill for any leader. Emotional regulation is a term psychologists have employed to describe "[t]he processes by which individuals influence which emotions they have, when they have them, and how they experience and express these emotions."[6] These may be automatic or controlled, conscious or unconscious. Researchers have shown that various competencies are involved, "including restraining and controlling impulses, dampening down distress, effectively channeling negative affect, and intentionally eliciting and sustaining pleasant (e.g., pride) and unpleasant (e.g., anger) emotions, when appropriate."[7] In the workplace, regulating emotions may involve actions like inhibiting personal desires and impulses. In the most successful organizations people work to help one another manage their emotions by influencing and effectively communicating with others.

James Gross has written the authoritative work on emotional regulation by setting out a number of emotion regulatory processes. These processes are described as follows:[8]

- *Situation Selection*: involves approaching or avoiding certain people or situations based on their likely emotional impact. It requires understanding what situations make you emotional, and may require the support or care of others.
- *Situation Modification*: involves active conscious efforts to modify a situation to alter its emotional impact. This differs from unconscious emotional expressions, which may modify a situation as well.
- *Attentional Deployment*: involves strategies to alter attentional focus of a situation, using processes of distraction, concentration, and rumination. Distraction focuses attention on nonemotional aspects of a situation. Concentration can absorb cognitive resources and even draw attention to emotional triggers. Rumination focuses attention on feelings and their consequences.
- *Cognitive Change*: involves reevaluating a situation to determine capacity to manage it to determine if emotions can be altered. This may involve reframing a negative situation more positively, denying a situation, or reappraising a situation to alter its impact.
- *Response Modulation*: refers to an alteration of the physiological, experiential, or behavioral response to a situation. This occurs late in the emotion regulation process and may include positive activities (e.g., exercise, relaxation, or biofeedback) or negative responses (e.g., alcohol, drugs, cigarettes, or eating).

Gross's five processes will take any leader time to master, but they encompass many ideas expressed by the leaders with whom we worked. They begin with having an understanding of what makes you anxious, and then move through a series of strategies to help you regulate your typical reactions. Such a process closely relates to ideas we discuss as lessons later in this chapter. And related to our objective to assist leaders with their emotional planning, Gross also suggests the development of regulatory goals to support individuals in learning to accomplish their personal emotional regulation. Setting such goals is seen as a means for helping people to appraise their own capacity for emotional regulation. Note Gross's description of these goals:

> What are typical emotion regulatory goals? Individuals often seek to decrease negative emotions and increase positive emotions. For example, flight attendants limit hostile feelings toward unpleasant passengers, and college students enhance positive feelings by social sharing. These goals are readily understood in hedonistic terms: people are motivated to avoid pain and seek pleasure. But emotion regulation is broader than a simple hedonistic account suggests. Emotion regulation

also involves increasing or initiating negative emotions and decreasing or stopping positive emotions. For example, bill collectors may increase their anger to help collect delinquent accounts, and the bearers of bad news may limit positive emotions as they deliver their unwelcome news. An empirical account of individuals' emotion regulatory goals is sorely needed. Such an account would permit a more complete analysis of the costs and benefits of different forms of emotion regulation as they are used in the service of various goals. This analysis also would help shed light on how factors such as fatigue and mental load differentially compromise an individual's ability to achieve specific regulatory goals.[9]

We concur with Gross about the importance of establishing goals. We believe that developing a mastery of handling emotional interactions requires leaders to know themselves and set goals to sharpen their evolving skills. Gross clearly emphasizes how important this is.

Regulating your emotions shares many characteristics with processes that researchers have identified for managing job-related stress. We believe that stress reduction strategies should be part of an overall plan for regulating emotions. Drawing from prior research on stress, Matthews et al. offered three practical tips for managing stress:[10]

1. Keeping an Emotional Diary: workers should spend a few minutes every morning clearing away frustrations and writing morning notes. Writing down whatever is felt, such a log or diary can be used throughout the day.
2. Using Humor: seen as perhaps the best medicine for dealing with stress, humor can act as a distraction from whatever is causing stress. The idea of creating a humor-filled environment is offered as a useful strategy, along with trying to view coworkers or the boss in funny rather than serious ways.
3. Using Mental Imagery: involves visualizing ourselves in different situations and outcomes. By identifying, refining, and practicing steps to be taken to achieve success, it becomes easier to carry these steps out in real life.

Learning how to regulate your emotions and manage work-induced stress can be useful for dealing with the emotions that will likely emerge as part of being in charge. Of course, not everyone likes to write their thoughts out, bring in humor as a distraction, or work to visualize ways to improve. But it is clear that our leaders expressed many of these same ideas through the stories they shared with us. From our perspective, taking account of your emotional skills, developing a set of regulatory goals as part of developing an emotional regulatory account, and identifying stress reducers that work for you (like the keeping of an emotional diary, using humor, or some form of mental imagery) can be part of a successful planning process.

EMOTIONAL COMPETENCE

Emotional regulation is just one part of a larger concept that focuses on the many skills that individuals can master in dealing with their emotions. Emotional competence is a term that has been closely linked to emotional intelligence. Like other forms of intelligence, emotional intelligence is seen by many as an ability or mental capacity that can be measured. Others, however, differentiate this intelligence from a set of emotional skills and knowledge that can be attained to function effectively in a wide variety of situations. This is the concept referred to as emotional competence, which captures an understanding of the skills needed to adapt to and cope with one's social environment. In contrast with constructs like intelligence, which are depicted as an innate ability, emotional competence is construed as a set of skills that are learned. Accordingly, there may be no relationship between one's emotional competence and one's actual emotional performance, as a variety of factors (e.g., motivations, values, or goals) may impact emotional reactions. So developing emotional competence skills, while significant, is no guarantee for workplace success, since these skills may not always be applied appropriately. But becoming skillful in emotional competence increases the likelihood that a leader will be able to deal with difficult emotional situations that will emerge. As researchers have emphasized, "rather than being pre-occupied with perceived threats and self-defeating attitudes, a person with well-developed skills of emotional competence is able to mobilize resources to gather new information, to acquire new insights, or develop further his or her talents."[11]

In the popular press, Dan Goleman has been the leading proponent of the importance of emotional competence, suggesting that it assumes a range of competencies that can lead to outstanding performance at work.[12] For Goleman, being emotionally intelligent is not enough. Learning emotional competencies is required to translate the emotional intelligence into job-related capabilities. Goleman's four domains of emotional intelligence include twenty competencies. These twenty competencies, listed by domain, include:

- *Self-Awareness*: emotional self-awareness, accurate self-assessment, and self-confidence.

- *Self-Management*: emotional self-control, trustworthiness, conscientiousness, adaptability, achievement drive, and initiative.
- *Social Awareness*: empathy, service orientation, and organizational awareness.
- *Relationship Management*: developing others, influence, communication, conflict management, visionary leadership, catalyzing change, building bonds, teamwork, and collaboration.

These twenty emotional competencies, once mastered, are seen as adding value to performance in the work setting. As we learned from our data and have tried to emphasize throughout this book, we are all very different, so no list of ideas will work for everyone. Each of us must shape his or her own skill-set given our personal strengths and weaknesses. So while we believe that Goleman and his associates identify useful competencies, we submit that every leader must tailor competency skills to their needs. Some, for example, who are very self-aware, may extract themselves from certain situations due to their inability to cope well, and instead have others step in who are better suited for that particular situation. Whether dealing with emotional issues or anything else, this is what good leaders do. But it begins with a good sense of yourself.

In the broader context of human development, Carolyn Saarni has identified a series of emotional competencies that include the skills and knowledge that individuals can attain to function adequately across situations. Indeed, her work draws from research on the emotional competencies developed from infancy through adulthood, and shows how deficits can contribute to emotional difficulties and behavior problems for children and adolescents. We see her ideas as very basic for developing a good plan for dealing with your emotions. Eight competencies are identified in her work that fall into three broad categories. Emotion expression is the range of affect that you communicate in any social interaction. Emotion understanding involves the knowledge developed about emotional experiences. Emotion regulation encompasses the ways in which you manage your emotions in interactions with others and in trying situations. The eight skills of emotional competence Saarni identifies include:[13]

(1) Awareness of your emotional state.
(2) Skills in discerning and understanding others' emotions.
(3) Skill in using the vocabulary of emotion and expression in terms commonly available in your subculture.

(4) Capacity for empathetic and sympathetic involvement in other's emotional experiences.

(5) Skill in realizing that inner emotional state need not correspond to outer expression, both in yourself and in others, and the ability to grasp that your emotional expression can impact others.

(6) Capacity for adaptive/coping with aversive or distressing emotions by using self-regulating strategies that may ameliorate the intensity of a particular situation.

(7) Awareness that the nature of any relationship is in part defined by the degree of emotional display and the degree of reciprocity in the relationship.

(8) Capacity for emotional self-efficacy—you view yourself as feeling the way you want to feel. You accept your emotional experience that is in alignment with your individual beliefs about what constitutes desirable emotional balance.

In our eyes, Saarni's list of competencies are basic and leaders should assess their degree of development in each area. Successful leaders are likely to have mastered these competencies, and any leader should reflect on himself or herself and consider plans to personally develop.

These various lists of emotional competencies offer valuable ideas for consideration when developing a plan for what you should address in preparing and honing the skills you'll need to be successful when you are in charge. If it is true that a high degree of emotional intelligence is significant for success as a leader, then mastering these competencies will prove very beneficial as you navigate through the emotional waters of making tough decisions.

EMOTIONAL AWARENESS

Possessing the ability to be fully cognizant of your emotions and the impact that they may have on you and others would seem to be a vital part of any emotional planning scheme. The concept of emotional awareness, while part of the notions of emotional regulation and emotional competence already discussed, has been set aside as a key skill related to occupational success. Goleman considers this a main ingredient of emotional intelligence in the workplace. But even years before emotional intelligence was identified, researchers had developed scales for measuring emotional awareness, what was seen as a cognitive skill that was defined as the ability to recognize and describe emotions in oneself and others. In this framework, having greater emotional awareness—information about your emotional state—was suggested as enhancing potential for success. Five hierarchically arranged levels of emotional awareness were depicted: physical sensations, action tendencies, single emotions, blends of emotions, and blends of emotional experience.[14]

The studies done on emotional intelligence and related concepts have suggested a number of competencies related to emotional awareness. Gerald Matthews and his colleagues provide an apt description of these competencies:

> accurately identifying the specific emotion one is experiencing; understanding how the emotion is related to one's goals and values; realizing how the emotion is linked to one's thoughts and behaviors; and appreciating how the emotion likely affects accomplishment. Emotional awareness is claimed to serve as a guide in fine-tuning on-the-job performance, including, accurately gauging the feelings of those around us, managing our unruly feelings, keeping ourselves motivated, and developing good work-related emotional skills.[15]

If you possess such skills, you are likely to be more self-reflective, have a greater appreciation of your abilities, and therefore will be more inclined to take appropriate actions to enhance success. As most of us have witnessed in friends, colleagues, or loved ones, there are times when a reaction to something far exceeds what normally should have happened . . . that something else is going on in that individual that causes him or her to erupt way out of proportion to the instigating event. As one of the leaders in our research, a superintendent, described to us, "My husband will ask at those moments, 'OK, what's going on. You shouldn't be this upset. Why this reaction?' " The leader with high levels of emotional awareness likely doesn't project the bottled up feelings about something else to a precipitating event that regularly would be handled with much more calm and ease.

In many fields, the opportunities for emotionally challenging situations are quite frequent. This may be due to unpredictable events like changes in leadership, takeovers, or budget cuts, or may just be the nature of the work in a particular field. It intuitively makes sense that developing a high level of emotional awareness can be beneficial to the leader having to deal with constant emotionally laden situations. In the nursing field, for example, where client demands, management concerns for cost efficiencies, scarce resources, and dealing with ill patients can create a physically and emotionally demanding workplace for caregivers, having high levels of emotional awareness would likely be a significant benefit for any practitioner. Joan Vitello-Cicciu offers five strategies to enhance emotional awareness for nurse leaders:[16]

1. *Keep an emotional reflection journal*: Described as a form of taking your emotional temperature, this involves keeping some sort of record to allow one to reflect on current feelings or prior emotions. It provides an opportunity for further retrospection about emotional responses that were troubling.
2. *Meditate daily*: Meditation can help anyone become more aware of how emotions affect you. It is especially recommended for preparing oneself for a potentially emotionally draining interaction.
3. *Engage in positive visualization*: Involves rehearsing in your mind difficulties that will be faced and how best to perform at the highest level. This is recommended for the preparation involved before a difficult encounter with a staff member. It also is recommended to help you imagine scenes of exemplary leadership.
4. *Use appreciative inquiry*: A process of discovering an individual or organization's strengths including an outcome of statements about where that person or organization wants to be in the future. It involves four phases: discovery (what is); dreaming (what might be); design (what should be); and destiny (what will be).
5. *Practice emphatic listening*: Pay attention to what others are saying, trying to understand issues from their perspective no matter how different their response might be from your own. Learn the reality of the other people you are dealing with, seeking validation of what they are saying (e.g., Is this what you mean?).

Many of these skills are aspects of what the proponents suggest are ingredients for becoming an emotionally intelligent person. Some reflect things our leaders discussed with us, like writing in a journal or finding time to meditate. Certainly, not everyone will desire to do all these things, though we would agree that learning to listen well should be basic for any leader hoping to succeed. But without getting into the debate about the veracity of emotional intelligence as a separate construct, we do believe that developing your emotional awareness is a distinct essential step for dealing with the emotional situations you will face as a leader. Developing emotional awareness must be part of your emotional planning.

EMOTIONAL BLUEPRINT

For purposes of preparing yourself for the emotionally laden future your organizational leadership will entail, the most useful work derived from the development of the idea of emotional leadership is detailed in David Caruso and Peter Salovey's book, *The Emotionally Intelligent Manager.* The book pulls from the research on emotional intelligence to build what they call the emotional blueprint. They describe it this way:

> We believe that it is difficult, yet possible, to become an emotionally intelligent manager. At first, learning to identify and use the data in feelings might be somewhat awkward and mechanical. It might seem like following a difficult schematic diagram or a set of instructions for assembling a complex machine. Whereas some of us learn the underlying principles over time and can dispense with detailed assembly instructions, others of us will always need the schematic or explicit steps. The good news we offer all managers is that we have developed a schematic for emotions—a set of detailed, how-to instructions. We call this an Emotional Blueprint.[17]

As we pointed out in Chapter 2, little empirical research has verified the veracity of or the predictive capabilities of the specific components of emotional intelligence. But work is progressing in the area, and our research suggests that the issues identified in the emotional blueprint resonate well with the specific concerns the leaders we worked with identified. So we offer the Caruso and Salovey blueprint as yet another strategy to aid in your emotional planning.

The emotional blueprint is composed of four steps that can be considered a problem-solving approach with an emotional focus. The first step is to *accurately identify emotions.* This is a data-gathering phase where you must become aware of your own and others' emotions. These are both verbal and nonverbal, and it will require some skill to distinguish between genuine emotions and expressions and forced emotions and expressions. The goal is to get complete and accurate data. For you as leader, this will require asking many questions, and paraphrasing back to others to be certain that you grasp what is being said and how your colleagues feel. Paraphrasing back what has been heard from someone else is a standard procedure employed by anthropologists to insure they understand what they are hearing.

The second step is to *use emotions to enhance thinking.* Emotions impact all of us, and this step calls for an examination of how and what we are thinking, which helps guide how we communicate with one another. This phase requires understanding what others are thinking and feeling, having empathy for others in learning to see the world through their eyes. This phase should result in the generation of a shared emotional perspective. The goal is to have feelings help guide your thinking. For leaders it involves a determination of how the various emotions and feelings influence your thinking and that of your workers.

Step three involves *understanding the causes and progression of emotions*. Emotions aren't random events, but instead have underlying causes. This step requires questioning to understand both the causes and the progression of emotions. There are always reasons that emotions erupt and evolve. It is the goal of this step to learn as much as possible about these emotional events and to evaluate possible emotional scenarios. For leaders it will involve examining the causes of the emotions and considering what might happen next.

Finally, step four is *managing emotions to achieve intelligent outcomes*. Strategic decisions should be based on understanding emotions and appropriate reasoning from that understanding. Emotions contain information that should help guide thinking. This step emphasizes the need to stay open to emotions and to develop actions based on knowledge about our and others' feelings. The goal here is to determine the underlying causes for emotional situations and to take appropriate action to solve problems. For leaders, this will require including both the more rational information that is available with the emotional data collected and analyzed to make the best decision.

We find the blueprint a very powerful approach to emotional planning. Our research suggests that the first step (identifying emotions) and the last step (managing emotions) are the keys to begin with when developing a plan for personal growth. Without the ability to handle these processes a leader is unlikely to succeed when emotional interactions occur. That said, we do find very useful the series of questions and exercises to help develop all four steps of the emotional blueprint, which Caruso and Salovey offer in the Appendix of their book. As they suggest, not every leader goes through every situation using this step-by-step approach. But they argue that emotionally intelligent leaders think about problems this way. Their thinking is summarized as follows: "the world of emotion is complex and confusing, but the emotional blueprint can help you navigate your way through the turbulence."[18]

LESSONS FOR PLANNING YOUR EMOTIONAL FUTURE

All the information we've discussed in this chapter offers you ideas for developing your personal emotional plan. There is a great deal of overlap among the various ideas we've set out, and we also learned from the leaders with whom we worked. Together these data suggest a series of lessons to consider as you begin the process of planning for your emotionally laden future. We like to think of these as our Emotional Dirty-Dozen!

Lesson #1—Accept that leadership involves emotional experiences. Much like death and taxes, we can guarantee that you will confront emotionally laden experiences once in a leadership role. They may be sporadic though some are predictable. But rest assured that they will happen, and the first step in preparing to deal with this is to accept this reality. We learned from the leaders we spoke with that many were taken back as they never anticipated the heavy emotional toll that making decisions would have for them. Others learned that even doing what they knew was the right thing didn't necessarily reduce the emotional toll they experienced. Having done what was right helped them deal with the emotional tension after a difficult decision or situation. But it didn't erase the uneasiness they felt. Our caution is simple here. Get ready.

Lesson #2—Be Prepared. The Boy Scout motto is especially appropriate for leaders. Once you accept that emotions will invade your world when you make decisions as a leader, then it is contingent upon you to get yourself prepared. We're reminded of the old saying that when you drive a car over a cliff, your options are severely limited. In this light, if you are ill prepared for the emotions that you'll face, then you likely will have few options in dealing with a particular situation. Remember Smokey the Bear's admonition that only you can prevent forest fires? Similarly, the onus is on you to get ready for the emotions you'll deal with as the boss. A part of your preparation should be to thoughtfully consider how you would behave in any personal interactions before they happen. We understand that there may be some instances where interactions are spontaneous. But in most situations that end up creating some emotional turmoil, there is an awareness of a meeting or interaction well in advance. This is where the ideas about visualizing how to behave can be useful. We also recall one leader, who was legally trained, who suggested that he was always guided by a standard often employed in court decisions— the *reasonable man* standard. In essence, this meant that he would consider how another reasonable person in the same circumstances might act, and he prepared how he would behave accordingly.

Lesson #3—Take Care of Yourself. This is one precaution about which these leaders were adamant. You need to make time for yourself, to identify the ways that you can diffuse the emotional strain when it hits. There are so many dysfunctional ways to go here such as heavy drinking, smoking, overeating, or taking your anger out on others. But there are many healthy and productive ways to behave as well. For some this may mean making time for exercise, getting away, taking long walks, or meditating. Several leaders we spoke with talked about the solace and clarity they discovered in writing things down, so keeping a journal or making emotional notes may help. Indeed, experts in positive psychology recommend writing as a process for achieving mental health.[19] All the leaders we talked to emphasized the importance of getting enough sleep. Some talked about the importance of having a good sense of humor as a means of helping to lighten their emotional load. "Laughter," one executive told us, "can be an incredible lift to the spirits." Several ideas we previously discussed about doing visualizations or mental imagery may be helpful. We consistently heard from the leaders about how they had developed what we consider their social ecologies by having supportive and helpful people as part of their world. These support networks may include friends, family members, a spouse, or professional colleagues. Some had mentors. Having a support network can clearly be an asset for any leader to rely upon. But the point of this lesson is to find what works for you, so you can take care of yourself.

Lesson #4—Become Emotionally Sensitive to Others. Anthropologists who study foreign cultures emphasize the importance of understanding the world from the perspective of those in that culture. It is the only way to truly appreciate why people behave as they do. As a leader you may be confused by the reactions to your decisions, but learning about other people's feelings will likely shed light on their behavior. Thus, this same cultural sensitivity that anthropologists employ can be applied to understanding the emotions of those with whom you work. You have to get into the shoes of those in your workplace to truly appreciate their reactions to you. This requires attending to the cues that others offer you about their behavior. It also requires listening carefully to what others say, what we previously identified as emphatic listening as an important means for understanding the emotional reality of those with whom you work.

Lesson #5—Be Aware of the Emotional Potholes. The stories, interviews, and conversations we had with leaders made one thing perfectly clear to us. There are certain types of individuals in any work setting and in all business/ professional relationships who may breed emotional angst for leaders. We largely dealt with these matters in Chapter 4, where we discussed the "high maintenance employees" with whom every leader has to work, as well as the myriad of issues that attend to working with friends once you're appointed to a leadership role. The lesson here is a simple caution...be aware of the potential for emotional fallout in dealing with such individuals. Recall the utter dismay that one of our leaders discussed in dealing with an obstinate colleague, where she was at her wits' end as to what to do given that she felt that she had been very giving and fair. Recall also the stories of problems that surfaced when leaders were in a position to supervise friends. We aren't suggesting any absolutes that must be avoided at all costs, but only that you be aware of the likelihood of problems in such situations and that you prepare yourself accordingly.

Lesson #6—Be Willing to Change. Several leaders cautioned about getting too stuck in your ways. They talked about how they had found a way to deal with emotional situations that worked, and tried applying that behavior in every situation they confronted. That didn't work. What they learned, and what is clear to us, is that leaders need to apply behaviors in each circumstance that fit the individuals and specific events in that circumstance. Economists talk about what they refer to as the *sunk-cost fallacy*. If monies have been invested heavily in a project that isn't working out well, should you continue to let the program unfold despite the problems and keep it going due to the large investments that have already been made? Or should you close the project down, accepting that the losses can't be recovered? President Bush appears to be struggling with the same reasoning regarding the war in Iraq. The argument is that pulling our troops out now would be an affront to the lives of those we've already lost in the war. The counter here, as it is in the economic example, is that it is better to cut losses now and move on to something more productive, as the lost costs are "sunk" and can't be recaptured. For leaders, getting too caught up in a single way of operating, perhaps because it is what you planned and the way you always have acted, is making the same mistake that the sunk-cost fallacy displays. The lesson is to change your behavior as is appropriate, be willing to try new ways to deal with employees. If you get too set in your ways of dealing with emotional issues, you may exacerbate rather than ameliorate any situation. Even if you've invested considerable time and energy already, a new and different approach may be in order.

Lesson #7—Own Your Expressions. Do you have a good poker face? Perhaps you watch poker players on television and note that many maintain the same expression whether they have good cards, are bluffing, or are uncertain of what to play next. Your expressions as a leader similarly are important. In Chapter 2 we discussed the research related to emotional labor and wearing the corporate mask, and presented some examples of this happening in the real world in Chapter 3. It can be heavy emotional work to maintain the right face for the company's sake, especially when the specific situation is one where you aren't certain exactly how to behave. There may be instances when it helps to display your true feelings, especially in those times when you are trying to show concern for someone. No matter the specific decision you make about how to express your emotions, a key will be to behave as honestly as you can. All of us give off cues as to how we really feel. Your expressions as leader have meaning. Be aware of the cues you are sending.

Lesson #8—Don't Panic. We live in a technology-supported world. We all appreciate that reality. Many interactions we have with employees come via e-mail. One leader warned about replying to messages electronically before you had taken the time to fully think through your response. She very emphatically told us, "Don't hit the send button until you are sure!" In generating replies to e-mails we get, we often send our response without carefully considering the impact of what we are saying. This same situation can happen in more traditional face-to-face or regular mail interactions, but the technology is so instantaneous today that responding quickly while in an emotional state is a real danger as it can heighten a problem that potentially could have been short-circuited with more careful thought and deliberation. Your urge to clarify or make the situation right is probably correct. Intuitively you may just want to move on to the next issue. But taking some care to think about what you are saying can prevent bigger problems from evolving, especially in a moment of emotional tension given the immediacy of e-mail. So the lesson here is simple—Don't panic, and don't hit the send button with your response until you are sure of what you want to say.

Lesson #9—Be Persistent. It is very easy for leaders to get frustrated and want to just give up. Coping with the emotional nonsense that leaders must deal with is hard. Recall the story we related about the leader whose wife urged him to give his role up because it was tearing him apart, only to be reminded by her husband that when he stopped feeling bad it would be time to quit. Nobody said that being in charge would be easy. It takes grit and determination to lead an organization well. A consistent message that came from our data was that dealing with the emotional side of leadership takes work and energy. But you have to stick with it and persist to do your job well. This, not surprisingly, is a component of success in any endeavor. Former President Calvin Coolidge was reported to have framed it this way:

> Talent will not; there is nothing more common than unsuccessful men with talent. Genius will not; unrewarded genius is almost a proverb. Education alone will not; the world is full of educated derelicts. Persistence and determination are omnipotent.

Perhaps if we had had the opportunity we could have convinced President Coolidge to add something about handling emotional issues as part of the success formula. But hanging in there and being persistent, constantly working on your emotionally related actions and reactions, is clearly a significant concern for any leader.

Lesson #10—Become Emotionally Aware. We firmly believe that you as leader cannot succeed unless you are fully aware of your emotions and are able to understand the emotions of the people in your work setting. Even the most heinous leaders throughout history understood this. Hitler was sophisticated in his use of propaganda as part of building up support for his leadership and the Nazi regime. Hitler was perhaps the first leader in the modern era who actually studied himself speaking on film so as to learn how to better orchestrate the emotions of his audiences. He knew all the right emotional buttons to push. His, of course, was a sick regime, but all leaders need to be aware of how they are feeling and reacting to people and how they affect others. The emotional competence of self- and social awareness are significant considerations for becoming aware of your emotions. The work to date on emotional intelligence is especially useful to help you with this. That research suggests that the most successful people are those with high levels of emotional intelligence. It requires being emotionally aware. There are instruments you can utilize to help you identify your emotional skills, which we briefly discussed in Chapter 2, such as Goleman's Emotional Competency Inventory, Mayer, Salovey and Caruso's MSCEIT, or the EQ Map developed by Cooper and Sawaf. Earlier in this chapter we provided some concrete ideas gleaned from the research on emotional awareness. The tools are out there, but you must put in the effort to become aware of your emotions and the emotions of others.

Lesson #11—Learn to Regulate Your Emotions. We found the research on emotional regulation to be very significant for leadership behavior. Clearly, becoming aware of your emotions and those of the people you interact with is part of being able to regulate your emotions. But there is more to it! Awareness alone without some requisite action to regulate those emotions is rather useless. The two emotional competencies of self- and relationship management are part of what needs to be considered. Gross' research on emotional regulation offers a clear set of guidelines to assist you with developing strategies for figuring ways to become proficient in regulating your emotions. Indeed, several lessons we've already offered can be part of a plan for developing your ability to regulate your emotions. But for our purposes, it is clear that being able to regulate your emotions will make it easier for you to deal with the emotional issues that will pervade your world as a leader.

Lesson #12—Develop Your Personal Emotional Plan. We close with what we consider the most important lesson of all. It is all-encompassing of the other lessons we've offered, and something that none of our leaders had ever undertaken. We argue that you need to develop a plan for how you will deal with the emotional side of being a leader. We want to force you to think about this easy-to-overlook component of leadership. The emotional blueprint presented by

Caruso and Salovey is a great starting point. The four steps involved with the blueprint—identify, use, understand, and manage emotions—provide a clear thought process for anyone dealing with emotions that should become a part of the way you approach your leadership role. But for our purposes, we believe that leaders should write out an outline of how they plan to become an emotionally sophisticated leader. Forcing you to write this out makes it more likely to become a part of how you behave. You should include several components:

1. How do you normally react to emotional situations? Think about your intuitive or gut reactions, and try to consider in what circumstances such reactions may work, and in what situations you will need to respond differently.
2. Set out your goals. What are the things you hope to accomplish in establishing your plan? Set targets for your behavior (e.g., not hitting the send button in replying to e-mails before you are ready, not raising your voice in discussions or yelling at workers, not reacting immediately unless it is an emergency situation, etc.).
3. What data will you need to collect when there is an emotional reaction so you can respond accordingly? Help yourself in reacting to emotional situations. Set out the things you feel you will need to fully understand before reacting. Probably most important here is to try to understand the perspective of the others involved in the situation.
4. Are there areas of your work, rules, or regulations that you need to learn more about? Are there any personal things you want to work on to improve your reactions?
5. Establish the exact steps you will take to achieve the goals that you've set out.

Gross's idea of an empirical account of emotion regulatory goals fits in with our thinking about establishing an emotional plan. You should develop your plan accepting that it will only work for you. It is geared to help you with the issues you need to focus on. Once you realize what you'll be facing as a leader, you should prepare yourself for the tasks ahead. Emotional planning is a new idea, but we guarantee it will have big payoffs.

CHAPTER 7

Epilogue

The human side of leadership sounds more like a war zone than a typical business, industry, health, or educational organization. Yet, that is what we found when we asked leaders to describe the emotionally charged challenges they faced on their watch; emotional challenges their prior training, education, and experience left them feeling ill-equipped to handle. One might wonder why did I or why would I decide to accept organizational leadership responsibility? There are many answers to that query. Most, however, center on a deep commitment to our peers, colleagues, and employees coupled with a sincere belief that as leaders we can make a difference in the organization's culture. We will not mislead you, reader, into thinking each story shared in "The Eye of the Storm" and "Extra Grace Required" had a storybook ending, nor even a civil and acceptable ending. However, we would like to share endings to a few stories that complete the respective leadership process.

Dr. Batcher was the college president wearing the "company mask" for his board and the board's legal counsel. Walking the litigious minefield ended in terminating five long-term faculty members whose college tenure ranged from twelve years to twenty years. Through formal state administrative hearing processes, civil court, and finally the appellate court, these cases dragged on for over two years. The final appellate court ruling was decided in favor of the college, and it was delivered as a new academic year began. The wounds were still fresh across the campus as the five loved colleagues were missed. It would have been easy for Dr. Batcher to "hunker down" to put the whole affair to rest. But he knew it would not go away and at least now he could remove the "company mask" and begin the healing. He knew he could help create a better environment for the students as well as all who worked at the institution. He began by concentrating on the five former colleagues' needs.

Early the next week following the appellate decisions, Dr. Batcher contacted three large, nationally recognized colleges and explained the reduction in force that had occurred. He then asked if it would be possible to consider these five faculty members for full-time faculty positions at their respective institutions. All three colleges agreed to fly representatives to the campus to interview the five faculty members. The stir created when these college representatives arrived on campus was palpable. In addition, the campus responded warmly to their five colleagues who came on campus for the interviews. Having the interviews on campus was a conscious decision on Batcher's part. This was to be an open and transparent attempt to provide whatever assistance the college could to helping faculty who through no fault of their own lost their positions. It was a gutsy call but one that met with positive acclaim, and while not all five wanted to relocate, the effort Dr. Batcher extended to these five colleagues did not go unnoticed by the campus. Nor, however, was it enough to change the residual climate within the culture or the culture itself. Dr. Batcher decided he needed to deal with these immediate residual feelings with which the campus community was dealing and having the five revisit the campus for the interviewing process gave him an idea.

It was late October. The college had no social events planned until mid-December and that was simply too far away to help bring healing. Besides, after the December events faculty would disappear for a month and there would be no legitimate opportunity for healing. Batcher said he believed something needed to be done and done quickly so that all could acknowledge the campus "elephant." He initiated the President's Thanksgiving Potluck. He provided and cooked four huge turkeys and asked all who came to bring a favorite Thanksgiving side dish. One week before the event he personally went to a close friend of each faculty member who left through the reduction in force and asked if he or she would be willing to give a short testimonial to the contributions made to the college by the departed faculty member. The hurt was so deep that in some cases Batcher had to make several solicitations, but he found someone to speak on behalf of each former faculty member.

The President's Thanksgiving Potluck arrived and though well over 300 faculty and staff were invited, seventy-five made the appearance. The Potluck began with a moment of silence held for private reflection and gratitude. Then President Batcher asked each faculty representative to present the prepared tributes to the five former faculties. It was a bittersweet

Thanksgiving meal, but it helped validate the grieving process that had been consuming people privately.

But Batcher's story did not end there. He said there was an unexpected surprise at the end of the meal. The five faculties who had made the toasts to their former colleagues approached Dr. Batcher and proposed that the President's Thanksgiving Potluck be an annual event. Furthermore, they suggested that any and all who left the institution during the next twelve months, be they faculty, staff, or administrator, and for whatever reason they may have left have a spokesperson provide a similar toast to the ones presented that year. In this way they felt that something positive would carry on in remembrance of this tragic reduction in force.

President Batcher held this event each year for the next seven years that he remained with the college. Each year the numbers grew. In fact the year after he left, the toast honoring his departure was heard by over 450 faculty, staff, and administrators. At this writing the tradition continues, and does so in spite of not having to have implemented another reduction in force.

In our conversations with President Batcher it became clear that wearing the "company mask" was an irritant to him; yet, it was also something he felt that he was required to do. His actions responding to the faculty reduction in force were reasons he accepted leadership responsibilities. He knew he could make a difference and create environments that would be nurturing to employees, while simultaneously allowing the institution to meet and exceed its mission and strategic goals. Entering an organization that had problems limited him and other leaders like him in terms of what could be done quickly to address the situation. In some cases this could mean fighting the battle to terminate an employee who is recalcitrant, unrepentant, and causing cultural chaos. But Batcher grew from the experience, and something positive came out of a horrendous situation.

You met Frank in "Extra Grace Required." One myth encountered concerning the business culture is how easy it is to let people go when they are causing organizational problems. Frank was hired to bring his particular division into line with company production and sales forecasts. He thought he had a superstar in Sam because his sales numbers were among the division's top each quarter. But that soon became clouded when he learned more about the personality behind the sales numbers. The upper-level vice presidents also were aware that Sam's numbers were among the division's best, but like Frank they were not aware of the personality behind the numbers. Remember, Frank was concerned that the vice presidents would balk if he took disciplinary action on Sam's antics. Frank told us that he had no data to support that feeling, but said he operated as though it were fact for much longer than he would like to admit. Frank shared that he also was concerned that there were many who found Sam so charming; yet, when problems occurred, the trail always led back to Sam.

Frank discussed his perceptions concerning Sam and his behavior within the divisional culture with nonpositional leaders to try to understand why there was such support for Sam. It became clear rather quickly that Sam was a bully to everyone in one way or another. To those who were below him on the organizational chart, he did not attempt to hide his disdain. To sales peers, he simply threatened them individually. When another sales staff member was close to breaking Sam's monthly sales record, Sam threatened to disclose the staff member's expense padding. While the staff member vociferously denied any such occurrence, Sam retorted, "Who will they believe? You or me?" The staff member became mysteriously ill the last week of the sales quarter, and Sam's record stood firm.

Having completed his information gathering, Frank approached the vice president to whom he reported directly and laid out the full scenario. Frank maintained that while Sam may be a top producer, the rest of the division was not operating effectively or efficiently because of Sam's behind-the-scene antics. The vice president refused to go as far as approving Frank's plan to terminate Sam, but he did not stand in the way. He simply warned that the sales figures had better not drop or there would be some hard questions concerning Frank's worth to the company for Frank to answer.

Frank went to his human resources specialist and discussed what possible support measures might be available to Sam to help him curb his bullying behavior. Having been thoroughly briefed on what was available, Frank also asked what steps he needed to take in terminating Sam should the support activities not be well received. Being forearmed, Frank tried to catch Sam that afternoon. He realized that on Friday afternoons many took an early leave, so he held little hope that he would be able to visit with Sam before the weekend. While that made for another restless weekend, it also provided Frank more time to think through what approach he would take and what personal and professional boundaries he wanted in place during the talk.

Early Monday morning, he contacted the Human Resources Director and asked that she attend the meeting for support and confirmation of Sam's reaction and decision. Frank was prepared to give Sam until the end of the week, Friday, to make his decision. He felt well-prepared in terms of his data gathering, the support services that would be available, and the boundaries he had established. It was now time to have the meeting and make his final decision.

Sam was surprised by the meeting and the fact that the Director of Human Resources was present. He vacillated between being ingratiating to condescending to finally his truer pattern, threatening and bullying.

There is no way in hell that I am going to accept the support services you are offering or even admit to your accusations for that matter. Just try and fire me and just watch how fast your vice president reverses that decision. You will be the one looking for a new job, not me.

Sam made it an easy call. Frank and the HR director provided the severance letter and security walked Sam to his office to watch him as he packed his belongings.

Frank told us he never inquired as to whether Sam made good on his threat and contacted his vice president. But Frank did have numerous meetings with his vice president to try and explain the division's upsurge in sales. In addition the camaraderie within the division was changed for the better. Laughter and goodwill had returned and few had realized how the workplace climate had eroded. Frank said he reflects on how other scenarios would have played out. What if he had taken to heart and believed Sam's statements concerning his leadership ability? Would he have made himself ineffective? What would have happened to his division had he allowed Sam to stay and continue to bully people in private? Frank is pleased these questions are but moot points. But when we asked Frank what made him turn the corner and decide to confront the bully head-on, he is not sure. He felt that there was no one culminating moment, but that it just seemed about time that he took some action.

Repairing the cultural climate and sometimes the culture itself is a common occurrence when emotional juggernauts are untangled openly for all to understand. Sometimes it means dropping the company mask; other times it means confronting the hierarchy and bringing its members out of denial; and at other times it means walking in where angels fear to tread. Such was the case when Franklin finally had reached the point where he knew he needed to act even in the face of upper-level administration and their respective legal counsel warning against such action.

Remember Franklin had confronted Danno on several occasions concerning his drinking and sexist behavior. During these confrontations he received no support from either legal counsel or from the Human Resource professionals. But Franklin was determined that something must be done, so he made one more visit to the Human Resources department and then on to legal counsel. In both instances he was told that an employee merely having alcohol on his breath did not constitute reason for administrative action. The turning point would be when the employee was unable to function and meet his responsibilities. Franklin knew this was a legalistic "cop out" that protected the rear ends of the administration and showed no care or concern for either Danno or whomever Danno may run over in a drunken blackout. But Franklin made up his mind that there would be a confrontation. It happened sooner rather than later.

Evening classes are popular with advanced graduate students, and Danno was a popular teacher during these late-night sessions because his sense of humor and informal style seemed to keep people alert. There were also stories that his coming to class after drinking led to crude "male sexist humor" at the expense of the women in his classes. However, all was overlooked or not reported since the "power equation" was in Professor Danno's favor. In other words, many students are hesitant to report perceived inappropriate professional behavior for fear of retribution. There had been rumors off and on concerning Danno showing up fairly intoxicated on several occasions. Now Franklin wanted to see how true those rumors were, so he simply stayed a little later on the nights Danno was teaching.

Eight weeks into a semester Dean Franklin was sitting in his office when a faculty member stuck her head in and said that there was a report that Danno had just come in smelling strongly of alcohol, laughing loudly, and slurring his words. With a quick, silent prayer for guidance, Dean Franklin asked the faculty member to accompany him and off they went to Danno's office. The Dean knew he had about thirty minutes before class to make a decision and a statement that he felt needed to be made. Reaching Danno's office Franklin closed the door and confronted him. "Danno, this office reeks of alcohol, and I smell alcohol on your breath and clothing. What is going on?" Danno tried to regroup and to give some reasonable explanation for the smell; however, he became incoherent. He was unable to conceptualize and focus on the conversation. Turning to the faculty member who accompanied him, Dean Franklin asked if, in the faculty member's opinion, Danno was fit to carry out his instructional duties. Franklin knew what he thought but wanted independent confirmation from the faculty member. The faculty member responded to Danno and the Dean that he should not be allowed to teach because he was unable to carry out his responsibilities.

Dean Franklin looked at Danno, "Danno, you will not be teaching this evening. I am sending someone to cancel your class, and we will talk about the consequences of your behavior when you are more coherent." Danno glared at Franklin and tried to fire back an expletive, but was unable to get anything coherent to come out at first. Then Danno began to get up and said he was going home. Franklin blocked the door and told Danno that if he left the office and went to the parking lot, he would call 911 and report a drunken driver. He talked to Danno about how that scenario would play out. Franklin then explained the situation. Danno was unable to perform the duties for which he was hired and that legal action would now be filed unless he agreed to receive help for his substance abuse illness. Danno said he had a problem with alcohol and wanted help. He asked Franklin what he should do. Franklin asked him for his car keys and said he would drive him to a treatment center. Danno agreed.

Franklin smiled at us at this point in telling his story. "I'll bet you think it is over and Danno was taken into treatment. Not that easy." We realized more of the story was yet to unfold. Franklin said he knew that taking Danno to treatment that night would not get him admitted. The insurance and admission process would take several days. Still he wanted Danno to see the treatment center and its campus so that he would have a concrete image in his mind. He also knew that Danno would "come to" and probably resist a return unless other actions were taken. Franklin sat through the admission intake and the questions and answers that made up the intake interview. He then drove Danno home and asked him not to come in the next day but to get ready to come back to the treatment center as soon as he was cleared for admission. Still, Franklin knew that the intervention was not complete.

Early the next morning Franklin saw a glimpse of Danno heading down the hall for his office. Franklin waited several minutes and casually walked down to ask Danno what he was doing there. "I'm just here doing my job. Last night was just a misunderstanding, and I am here ready to give this job all I have." Franklin set a meeting with Danno for later that afternoon. He was not surprised but disappointed. He previously had scheduled morning meetings with both human resources and legal counsel to lay out a plan. He needed to find a way to help Danno, yet strengthen his own hand in bringing this matter to a conclusion. The meetings gave Franklin the legal parameters within which he could operate. In meeting with Danno later that afternoon he laid out the full extent of the options he had. He began the conversation:

Danno, I will always be here for you as a friend who cares about you and wants you to get well and to return to the college and be successful. However, please know that as Dean, I am here to protect this college and help it become stronger as well. Therefore, I will give you the opportunity to develop a personal treatment plan to present to me for my approval by tomorrow afternoon. If you choose not to take advantage of this opportunity, I will bring formal charges against you to the faculty committee and ask for your dismissal from the university. Those are the options I have at my disposal.

Danno responded in a characteristic fashion and said, "Well, I have options, too. And I will consult with people and my attorney to explore those options as well." To this Franklin replied,

> Danno, I understand you do have those options but please think carefully about what you hope to achieve by availing yourself of them. For if you choose to ignore the opportunity I am giving you to begin treating your alcoholic illness, I will file the paper work to have you terminated Monday morning. You have until tomorrow afternoon, Friday at 4:00 PM, to meet with me and discuss your plan.

The meeting ended in acrimony. The pleasantness was gone. The denial began to creep back into Danno's voice and actions. Franklin said that he believes a great deal in prayer as a way to help him focus his energies and to keep him "right sized" as he called it. He said that that afternoon and evening he spent time praying that Danno would accept the terms of the intervention.

Friday came and Franklin said he knew it would be the day of truth for both him and Danno. The word had spread quickly among faculty and students about the missed class and its cause. All eyes were on the dean's office to see what would happen next.

Danno appeared at 4:00 P.M. as decided. He looked angry and belligerent. Then he broke into tears. Knowing this pattern, Franklin remained unmoved. "What have you decided, Danno?" Franklin asked. "I'm going to the treatment center tomorrow morning. Admission called me today and they have a bed for me. I check in at 11:00 A.M." Franklin and Danno spent the hour going over the logistics of covering the classes, the announcement Danno wanted made at the faculty meeting, the insurance and leave paperwork, and the general anxiety and nervousness Danno had embarking on such a personal journey. They shook hands, and Danno was off to treatment.

Franklin said that it has not been long enough to know what the outcome will be for the long-term success for Danno. But he is not surprised that the faculty and student support has been so positive for what Danno is trying to do. Everyone seems to be pulling for Danno and grateful that this situation is now in the open.

Intervention strategies are not easy in a litigious society with weak administrative leadership hiding behind legalese and showing little concern for what can happen to people's lives. The friend mentioned in "Extra Grace" who spent twelve years in prison for vehicular homicide and the families of the young men he killed stand as a stark reminder in opposition to the "legal barons" within any organization. Finding a way around, through, or over the "system" to save the lives of our colleagues and employees and the innocent people they may touch tragically seems worth the chutzpah that it takes to break these cycles. But there are other benefits that Franklin sees in the path he took.

The college's general climate has changed dramatically when faculty and staff and even students saw how the illness of substance abuse could be handled compassionately and competently. This was so different from what they expected with the legal approach of finding the person unable to perform and then firing him. They also realized that dealing with these issues in a transparent way helped all understand not only what was happening and why but also what they could expect in terms of help for other issues they themselves might face. Acting decisively impacts more than just the main players in the drama. It is like tossing a pebble into a small puddle and watching the rings reach the other shore. It is often hard to know everyone whose life is touched in these interventions but Franklin said the risk was worth everything.

> This is a part of leadership . . . stepping up to the big issues that really affect the culture and the climate of an organization and reaching out to our colleagues who are hurting . . . walking in where angels fear to tread. It is all part of being a strong, yet compassionate leader.

It wasn't easy for Franklin, but in this case, doing what he knew was right helped.

Our leaders shared that they felt emotionally charged situations requiring decisive action always would be a part of the leadership landscape. Many acknowledged that even after the "main" event there were repercussions within the culture that they did not foresee. Throughout several stories there was either an implicit or explicit theme surrounding sexual harassment. While we have found that sexual harassment can target men as well as women, these leaders' experiences identified men rather than women and usually in power positions, as the harassers. Once these situations are resolved, the pain continues until additional leadership intervention occurs. We would like to highlight one such episode that was an undercurrent to several situations discussed earlier in the "Eye of the Storm" expanded here in the "Epilogue."

Charles was hired as a new corporate vice president, and while few understood the hiring process and even fewer were involved, the general consensus was that the company really found a true "go getter." Coming off a recent divorce, though no one knew if it were his first marriage or his third, he soon became a prize sought by single and some not-so-single women. Within weeks Charles made his selection and began openly courting Cathy, a single mother of two, who was also a division director for one of Charles's most important divisions. While there was some disappointment among the "contestants" who lost, the general mood seemed to be positive.

Most organizational cultures have rules, written and unwritten, about romantic entanglements within the workplace. While there have been crude little sayings surrounding office romance, most are more sage advice than even the participants want to believe. "Their" romance always is different and will last for all time. They imagine they are better as a "corporate team" than they are individually. Universally this is never the case and Charles and Cathy give us but one more example.

It wasn't long after the employees unofficially acknowledged the relationship that Cathy began carrying more decision-making weight than her divisional director position provided. She began first by giving what many perceived to be orders rather than ideas and soon was involved in major corporate decisions through her influencing Charles either in planning meetings or their "pillow talk." More than once other divisional directors became visibly upset as Charles would give his little smile to Cathy and agree with her stance often at their expense. Watching corporate resources flow to Cathy's division and not theirs became grist for the mill that Charles had lost his bearings on the company's objectives. It was here that the hostile environment, so often misunderstood and overlooked, took its foothold.

It wasn't long before Cathy merely had to mention an idea or criticism to another divisional peer and change was almost instantaneous. Many believed that even Charles was not aware of some of the directions Cathy had set for the company. All in all, many division directors felt constricted as they attempted to serve two masters. Cathy's power had become palpable, and only the uninitiated would argue it wasn't so. But Cathy's power was not the main concern; it was how she used and often abused that power to gain her own objectives. Her callous treatment of others became a cause for concern that soon reached Charles' direct report, the corporate president. It was also a behavior that Cathy's peers and subordinates would remember for a long time.

Charles's quarterly meeting did not go well. The news that he and Cathy were an item had subsided since it had been running for six months, but the business entanglements were becoming more pronounced and reaching the president's ears more frequently. President Tweedberry had been pleased he was able to hire Charles away from a competitor but now he was beginning to realize why that "steal" was so easy. He and Charles had a long discussion and the president attempted to convince Charles that there were other mates for him outside the company boundaries. Charles held firm. Cathy was the love of his life; he would leave the company before he would end this relationship. President Tweedberry sighed and asked that Charles at least move Cathy to a divisional satellite with different responsibilities to relieve some of the discomfort and outright disgruntlement her current positioning was causing. Charles agreed.

Cathy assumed her new role and was fairly well received. Her new colleagues were pleased to have Charles' ear in absentia. Cathy, though feeling she had been demoted, put on a brave front. She realized that she had lost her clout in major battles since she was now removed from the "real" corporate action. Her influence over Charles in their alone time dwindled considerably since she was no longer knowledgeable about what was happening at headquarters. President Tweedberry had made an astute move, and while Charles seemed unconcerned, Cathy was becoming less than happy.

Cathy's unhappiness was not solely related to her displacement and power reduction. She was beginning to see a side of Charles she had not witnessed before in their relationship. She now realized that Charles was a heavy drinker. What she wrote off before to celebratory drinking over their new relationship, new clients, new success goals, new power acquisitions, she was now seeing not as a partner in those events, but from the lens of a disenfranchised player and partner. When she confronted Charles concerning this behavior, he became abusive: first toward furniture and dishes and important pictures Cathy kept in antique frames, then the abuse turned on Cathy. It was verbal at first, but soon it became physical: grabbing her arm or pushing her down on the sofa or trying to push her down a flight of stairs. She tried to rationalize the behavior as something triggering Charles at work and pleaded to be brought back to headquarters to help him. Those pleadings made Charles angrier; he became more moody and sullen.

Cathy had a beachfront cabana that belonged to her parents, which she used often to get away and rethink difficult situations. She thought this might work for Charles as well and planned a romantic weekend getaway for the two of them. Charles showed up at the cabana drunk. Cathy tried to feed him and put him to bed, but he insisted on going to the liquor store first. It was a terrible weekend. Cathy received a black eye and a broken rib. She called the sheriff and pressed assault and battery charges.

On Monday morning Cathy went to President Tweedberry and laid out the abusive relationship, which included much more than the brief snippet recorded here. Tweedberry was not surprised. Since Cathy's relocation there had been other stories centering on Charles' drinking, carousing, and his sexually inappropriate comments to women inside and outside the company. Even Tweedberry's close friend and longtime customer called to ask whether the president was aware of Charles' actions. Unfortunately Tweedberry was not aware, but not surprised either. On Monday afternoon the corporate human resources vice president told the president that formal charges had been filed against Charles by two female employees. It was time to act, and Tweedberry called Charles in and relieved him of his responsibilities. The severance package Charles wanted was denied. Charles was sent packing that afternoon.

Having resolved the immediate crisis, President Tweedberry brought Cathy back to her divisional director position and waited for normalcy to return. But such was not to be. There is a misguided feeling that once the crisis has been resolved that no more attention is needed to correct the past hurts and injustices. What Tweedberry and Cathy did not realize is that many of Cathy's actions sanctioned by Charles were being resurrected and resented. Her callous and abusive treatment was not forgotten nor forgiven because it had never been recanted. Cathy was seen as a major antagonist and Tweedberry moving her to the satellite location confirmed their perceptions. Thus, when Cathy returned without any correction of past grievances, there was little relief experienced by those who had remained.

Cathy was stunned. She had expected a royal welcome upon her return, and she especially had expected that the women would rally around her to commiserate her plight. Cathy expressed her disappointment to Tweedberry, who advised her to continue her work and attempt to regain the professional respect and admiration she had earned before Charles had arrived. He even assigned her several projects that required her to work collaboratively across divisional lines to allow her the opportunity to make amends and regain her stature. It was far from what Cathy had expected.

It took two years for Cathy to regain her stature among her peers and subordinates. It was Cathy who shared this story with us after we had first interviewed Tweedberry. She was reluctant at first but called one of us one night and said that she wanted to share the story because she felt it would help her and others. Cathy said that the main leadership lesson she learned was that repairing a culture after a traumatic event was not easy. Like Tweedberry, Cathy felt that once Charles left, everything would return to the way it was before his arrival. She was unaware that she was being held responsible not only for her heavy-handed actions but also for many hurtful actions that Charles meted out to employees as well.

There were times in the two years that the healing took place that Cathy felt she was ostracized from social events that occurred among her colleagues. Baby showers, weddings, even Friday night gatherings occurring right after work were held without Cathy being invited. Even her office, once close to the other divisional directors, was moved so as not to be near them when she returned. We asked Cathy what she understood about her peers' actions. She said that she finally realized through some counseling, help, reflection, and making her own amends to those she felt she had hurt that she had been given time to heal. Going through the court system as she pursued her charges against Charles, reconnecting with her children and parents, working with Tweedberry to reestablish her role and responsibilities, all were part of her healing process. She had come to realize that while she had moved or perhaps grown from her victim role to one of healed person, her colleagues had not had that opportunity to heal and to bring a closure to the drama that had engulfed them unwittingly and unwillingly.

When we returned and asked Tweedberry what lessons he had learned having Cathy's permission to share her enlightenment, he thought a long time.

> I realized some, not all, of the hurt Cathy had been through, but I did not stop and think about what others might have experienced. I did not take the time to bring people together and help the healing process. I felt that "business as usual" would repair the damaged relationships. I didn't go beyond that nor did I ask my human resource professionals to assess how we might be proactive. As I recall now they did suggest some counter measures but I waved them off. It makes me wonder what image I project that they did not come back and push their case more strongly.

Over one year abusing the culture and two years trying to heal it. Still, the healing is nowhere near complete. Quite a price tag! When employees say, "We are adults, we know what we are doing," we sense that is equivalent to the scared six-year-old boy whistling as loud as he can while pedaling as fast as he can through a cemetery—all the while thinking in his mind that nothing bothers me, bothers me, bothers me. The lesson we suggested in the prior chapter about learning to appreciate what others are thinking really speaks to the issues here.

Sexual harassment is more than a control or power maneuver by one individual over another. Today there is more woman-on-man-harassment and same-sex harassment as well. It makes no difference if harassment turns into love or romance; what gets disturbed is the culture. Creating a hostile environment spills over to everyone and often affects those in the relationship least of all. But it is another leadership elephant that leaders first refuse to see and acknowledge and later refuse or are unable to determine the full extent of the damage done to the culture.

FINAL THOUGHTS

Being so grateful to all leaders, and those like Cathy to whom we went to learn follow-up stories, it seems only fitting that we tell a story on ourselves. We, the authors, never, from the book's outset, claimed to be the perfect or even model leaders; thus, we hope that you will learn from our errors as well.

Earlier in our careers, we, Rick and Tim, came to the same university at the same time. Tim arrived in June to teach a summer course before his full-time faculty appointment began and Rick arrived in August of that same summer as an administrator, the head of the division where Tim would be teaching. For some reason we hit it off from the beginning. There was a warmth and trust and respect in the relationship that included and acknowledged the past achievements each had earned. There was an open invitation between us to disagree, and to build together, and for five years this relationship continued to deepen and blossom.

Tim's responsibility was to develop a new doctoral program and by the end of the fifth year, with Rick's help, this program had achieved a national reputation. It was time to add to the faculty to help strengthen the program even more. Rick saw that and moved a new position into Tim's program a year or two earlier than was scheduled. By the following fall a new faculty member, Gibson, was hired who possessed not only a Ph.D. in the field but also a J.D., to help in teaching law. Gibson's first year was successful. He was and remains a wonderful addition to the program. Early in Gibson's second year a brief episode occurred that demonstrates how even strong friendships can get challenged.

Rick reported to an administrator who kept close tabs on what was happening in all the units that reported to her. Rick was often under pressure to accomplish goals though he was given leeway to carry out directives as he saw fit. He usually felt that he could manage through these without upsetting those faculty members who may be affected. In the majority of cases Rick was on target. But every now and then there would be a concern raised between Rick and his boss that did not get translated clearly to the faculty. Such was the case one fall after enrollment had been finalized.

Rick had been given certain targets to hit and felt assured that they would be. On a Saturday morning he walked by Gibson's office, and seeing the young professor working hard on a weekend, he casually inquired about how things were going. At some point he asked about the enrollment strength of his classes and the program. Gibson presented what was thought to be the enrollment, very pleased about what he had to report. But Rick, surprised about what he heard, became nervous and then unnerved. He made some comments about enrollment concerns given the mix of on- and off-campus students that Gibson had described.

In Jungian terms, Rick is an extrovert and he thinks out loud. As often as not he has better thoughts later but the first ones that arrive on the scene can drive fear into the hearts of the truly strong and noble. And so it was this Saturday morning as Tim received a concerned e-mail from Gibson wondering if it could be true that his new position might be in jeopardy based on the enrollment report that he had just shared with Rick.

Rick, interestingly, had no clue that his rambling thoughts might be interpreted this way. He was troubled about what was described to him concerning a planned enrollment mix of on- and off-campus students that Tim had developed and shared with Gibson, and made some very reactive comments about how poor on-campus enrollments can affect tenure decisions. He was thinking out loud about future hires, but his comments were understandably misconstrued by Gibson.

On the other hand, Tim couldn't believe Rick would intentionally put the fear of unemployment into anyone's heart. Yet, what the hell was he doing? Why would he even ask a fairly new-minted faculty member the questions he was when he could have asked Tim, his friend and program chair? E-mails flew back and forth that weekend between Rick and Tim as Tim tried to ferret out just what Rick's boss was after and what Rick thought he had found out. Rick was taken aback by what he felt was Tim's overreaction. Being unaware of how his remarks had been interpreted by Gibson and reported to Tim, he didn't feel as if he had threatened anyone and couldn't understand Tim's anger.

Finally, late Sunday evening, Tim sent the last e-mail, which in summary offered his resignation from the university and the less-than-hidden-threat that he could and would develop a similar program elsewhere. At this point Rick could have upped the ante and invited Tim to do just that but did not respond by e-mail. Through Rick's leadership he was able to stop the escalation of their disagreement and bring a calm to their exchanges. But Rick realized he had messed up by not considering the potential reaction to his less-than-well-considered remarks to Gibson.

Years later, when we, Rick and Tim, were beginning the emotional leadership research, we were presenting some data results and interpretations at a national meeting. We were asked to submit a chapter for a leadership book for the Open University in the United Kingdom. During casual conversation the contact asked whether any of the stories being shared at the conference were from personal experience. We assured him they were not and that they came from the leaders whom we had interviewed. He then asked whether we had any interactions between us that supported the theory-base we were developing. While we said "No," we were both thinking of this same incident. Later that evening Rick said that sometime we needed to talk about that incident because it so reflected what we were learning from others.

As we reflect back on that situation, we recall the situation thus: Tim couldn't believe that Rick would say the things he did, especially to a newer faculty member. He was outraged that Rick didn't come directly to him. Rick was completely surprised by Tim's reaction to his casual encounter with Gibson. He thought that Tim was overreacting to something he didn't fully understand. No doubt there is some truth to both observations. But the bigger question for us is what causes close business relationships and even friendships such as ours to even begin to head for such troubled waters? Uncertainty is a part of it, as we all can be affected by not knowing what is going on or by what might happen. But it is more than that. We believe that much of what has been shared with us about navigating emotions comes form a reservoir of fear: Fear of the unknown; fear of rejection; fear of success; fear of failure; fear of confrontation; fear of not being liked or pleasing everyone; fear of hurting someone, even yourself; or even fear of the future. As our leader told us from a story related in Chapter 6,

> . . . I learned that underneath people's ugliness, hostility, and nasty behavior there is fear. Fear of losing a job, fear of being rejected. Fear can take on so many disguises that I have learned always to look for that first in a really contentious situation.

Fear can spur you on to achieving great heights or cloud your thinking and lead you astray. It is regularly used in political campaigns to steer voters toward one candidate or away from another, and even has been depicted as a significant part of American society in Barry Glassner's book, *The Culture of Fear*.[1] Earlier we discussed the "flight or fight" response to threats, and fear certainly plays a part in that common reaction. The Indian spiritual leader Krishnamurti established fear as the movement from certainty to uncertainty.[2] Uncertainty promotes fear, and in leaders this can have toxic effects, if uncontrolled.

Certainly our psychologist friends will see this as just barely scratching the surface and might look to childhood trauma, early adult failures, and critical incidents that occur throughout our lifespan to put a finer point on the emotional reactions we find in the workplace. Clearly, this whole concept of fear as it affects leadership is fertile soil for future research. But for us a common ground upon which to begin might well be the advice our leaders gave us, and looking at the underlying fear or uncertainty even when we are unable to see it.

This is why we emphasize planning as we do. We recognized the need for emotional planning from the stories we heard and the conversations we held. We came to see our own shortcomings. Had Rick thought through his emotional reactions prior to the incident and had a plan, his interaction with Gibson would have been very different. If Tim had a plan for his emotional response the incident may not have escalated. But fear and uncertainty drove both of us. We had no plan. Along with creating some uncomfortable times associated with work, it almost cost us our friendship.

Years have passed since Tim and Rick shared that unsettling time together. They have moved on to different positions and are connected electronically rather than by footsteps down the hall. Still the friendship and the learning and the sharing of their respective workplace emotional challenges continue. Working on this book together has allowed us to share with those readying themselves for their own leadership journey: the trials and tribulations of seasoned veterans in the leadership field who took the time to study something that affected them. You will face these difficult situations, and with some forethought and planning you will succeed. You will learn to navigate your own and others' emotions as you value and respect the human side of leadership.

Appendix: Resources for the Interested Reader

After decades of ignoring the importance of emotions in the workplace, many scholars studying organizations and practitioners in business and other fields have begrudgingly accepted that emotions are worthy of their attention and study. Though the leadership literature remains rather meager on the topic, today there are journals dedicated to emotions, and popular concepts like emotional intelligence appear all across the research and public media landscape, with the promise of more studies on the way. Though this book takes a new perspective on the impact of emotions on those in leadership positions, the interested reader still has a wide array of sources to plow through if there is a desire to learn more about the topics associated with the human side of leadership. Our students and we read literally hundreds of books, articles, and book chapters covering a dizzying array of topics in preparing this book. Nobody need go through that pain, but there are key works that will assist the interested reader in becoming more familiar with these associated topics. We also recommend examining the many sources we've cited throughout the book for those wanting a more thorough understanding of the different material we covered.

What is clear to us is that we could easily prepare an entire volume discussing the materials and sources that helped shape our ideas. In the preceding chapter we purposely did not reference hundreds of worthwhile sources available on emotions and related topics, but rather focused on developing and presenting our research to make sure that the important ideas we raised are considered by those currently leading, hoping to lead, or preparing future leaders. That said, if one is inclined to spend time playing on the Internet, just Google "emotional intelligence" and you'll find nearly 2.8 million sites to spend the rest of your life plowing through! But for the adventurous reader, we offer the following brief synopsis of some of the more significant materials we uncovered, trying to avoid listing too many works that may be too technical for the nonacademic reader. We also provide some direction for those wishing to add the Internet sites available to their inquiry. We make no promise of being all-inclusive, so please understand that we are leaving out many wonderful sources in this short overview. And hopefully, interest in the topics we've addressed will grow and more scholarship will address the important issues in the future.

INTELLIGENCE

Psychologists have been fascinated with the construct of intelligence for about a hundred years. The literature on related concepts like emotional intelligence and social intelligence has grown in the past few decades. Below we list key works that assisted us in thinking differently about issues like intelligence and emotions.

- Gardner, Howard. *Frames of Mind: The Theory of Multiple Intelligences*. New York: Basic Books, 1983.

Gardner's work on multiple intelligences helped change the way that many people think about the entire construct of intelligence, arguing that there are varying intelligences that humans may possess. Others have written on related topics since, and Gardner himself has more recent works for the curious, but this is the place to start.

EMOTIONS

The works we relied most heavily on were very academic-oriented books and journal articles. Those listed below provided the needed background and insight to us on a number of issues related to the broad field of emotions. Today there are academic journals dedicated solely to examining this area, and the interested reader will have an abundance of material to cover. Here are some we recommend:

- Ashkansay, Neal M., Charmine E.J. Hartel, and William J. Zerbe, eds. *Emotions in the Workplace: Research, Theory and Practice*. Westport, CT: Quorum Books, 2000.

- Hochschild, Arlee R. *The Managed Heart: Commercialization of Human Feeling.* Berkeley, CA: University of California Press, 1983.
- Lord, Robert G., Richard J. Klimonski, and Ruth Kanfer, eds. *Emotions in the Workplace: Understanding the Structure and Role of Emotions in Organizational Behavior.* San Francisco, CA: Jossey-Bass, 2002.
- Plutchik, Robert. *The Psychology and Biology of Emotion.* New York: Harper-Collins, 1994.
- Rolls, Edmund T. *Emotion Explained.* Oxford: Oxford University Press, 2005.

These are all written for a scholarly audience. But the edited volumes cover a wide array of related topics; Plutchik's book and Roll's book provide a very thorough discussion of the concept of emotions, and Hochschild's book introduces the terms emotional work and emotional labor to the field.

EMOTIONAL INTELLIGENCE

The concept of emotional intelligence was introduced in the early 1990s by scholars John Mayer and Peter Salovey. But Daniel Goleman popularized the idea a few years later, and today there are literally thousands of books, articles, and Web sites examining the concept. No list we could generate would be complete given the popularity of emotional intelligence. Here are several of the key books we recommend:

- Ciarrochi, Joseph, Joseph P. Forgas, and John D. Mayer, eds. *Emotional Intelligence in Everyday Life.* 2nd edition. New York: Psychology Press, 2006.
- Cherniss, Cary, and Daniel Goleman, eds. *The Emotionally Intelligent Workplace: How to Select for, Measure, and Improve Emotional Intelligence in Individuals, Groups, and Organizations.* San Francisco, CA: Jossey-Bass, 2001.
- Goleman, Daniel. *Emotional Intelligence: Why It Can Matter More than IQ.* New York: Bantam Books, 1995.
- Goleman, Daniel. *Working with Emotional Intelligence.* New York: Bantam Books, 1998.
- Matthews, Gerald, Moshe Zeidner, and Richard D. Roberts. *Emotional Intelligence: Science and Myth.* Cambridge: A Bradford Book, MIT Press, 2002.
- Salovey, Peter and John D. Mayer, eds. *Emotional Development and Emotional Intelligence: Educational Implications.* New York: Basic Books, 1997.

Most of these works will be very readable to the lay audience. Goleman's works are written in an easy style and his influence is clear in the many volumes available on the topic. Matthews's book is very scholarly in orientation, but we include it as it represents the most thoughtful and critical analysis of the concept of emotional intelligence, both in terms of its current development and understanding. It is quite thorough in reviewing many of the claims made for emotional intelligence, but leaves a reader with a fuller understanding of its promise. We also recommend just a few journal articles that represent the thousands in the academic arena that have helped shape thinking about emotional intelligence:

- Dulewicz, Victor, and Malcolm Higgs. "Emotional Intelligence: A Review and Evaluation Study." *Journal of Managerial Psychology* 15 (2000): 341–372.
- Mayer, John D., and Peter Salovey. "The Intelligence of Emotional Intelligence." *Intelligence* 17 (1993): 433–442.
- Salovey, Peter, and John D. Mayer. "Emotional Intelligence." *Imagination, Cognition and Personality* 9 (1990): 185–211.

One last work that was recently published doesn't fit neatly into the categories of intelligence, emotions, or emotional intelligence but is certainly worth a look. Robert Sutton's book *The No Asshole Rule*, which we highlighted in Chapter 4, underscores the dilemma created by working with difficult employees. It emphasizes for us that difficult people can affect bosses, that difficult bosses can affect employees, and that difficult employees can affect other employees. As Sutton puts it, these assholes can negatively impact the work environment, and the book goes well beyond discussion of workplace bullying we referred to in Chapter 4. His easy-to-read book provided us with useful insights.

As previously indicated, there are literally thousands of Web sites dedicated to emotional intelligence. Here are several to get a reader started on examining the Internet. Several of the authors already cited have established Web sites associated with their research program or specific books:

- http://www.eiconsortium.org.

This is the Web site for the Consortium For Research on Emotional Intelligence in Organizations. The consortium publishes books, holds conferences, shares EI measuring instruments, and provides a lot of information for the interested reader. It also offers links to a variety of other Web sites related to the topic, and information on members like Daniel Goleman, Cary Cherniss, Reuven Bar-On, David Caruso, and other leaders in the field.

- http://www.csee.net.

This is the Web site for the Center for Social and Emotional Education. It is dedicated to providing materials and information for K-12 educators.

- http://www.emotionaliq.org.

A Web site with links to articles, workshops, certification, and the like, all related to emotional intelligence developed by John Mayer and Peter Salovey.

- http://www.unh.edu/emotional_intelligence.

Probably the most comprehensive Web site dedicated to Mayer and Salovey's work on emotional intelligence, this one was developed by Mayer at the University of New Hampshire.

- http://www.eq.org.

The EQ directory hosts links to information related to emotional intelligence. This site calls itself the most comprehensive of emotional intelligence-related sites, sources, and organizations. It offers quite an array of options for the interested reader.

- http://www.danielgoleman.info/blog/.

This is Daniel Goleman's Web site. It offers information on the many topics he has written on and his postings to his blog.

- http://ei.haygroup.com/resources/default_ieitest.htm.

Provides a nice introduction to the topic and an online test to get a sense of your own level of emotional intelligence.

LEADERSHIP

A thorough review or listing of the thousands of works published on leadership would be an immense undertaking. It is complicated by the fact that there is a literature on management, on leadership, on leadership for business, education, hospital administration, and other industry-specific fields. We won't begin to cover an examination of leadership with our list, but instead offer a number of sources that helped us move our thinking outside the traditional lines of inquiry in the field.

- Bolman, Lee G., and Terrence E. Deal. *Reframing Organizations: Artistry, Choice and Leadership*. San Francisco, CA: Jossey-Bass, 1991.

Bolman and Deal introduce the idea of different frames for examining organizations and leadership. Among the many contributions was including a political and symbolic frame to the organizational discourse.

- Cooper, Robert K., and Ayman Sawaf. *Executive EQ: Emotional Intelligence in Leadership and Organizations.* New York: Grosset/Putnam, 1996.

This book was among the first to bring ideas about emotional intelligence to the field of leadership. They offer what they call the EQ Map questionnaire to help leaders identify their strengths and vulnerabilities related to emotional intelligence.

- Caruso, David R., and Peter Salovey. *The Emotionally Intelligent Manager: How to Develop and Use the Four Key Emotional Intelligence Skills of Leadership.* San Francisco, CA: Jossey-Bass, 2004.

Another source bringing the research on emotional intelligence to the level of organizational management by two of the leading researchers in the field. The book offers ideas about understanding, developing, and applying emotional intelligence skills.

- Goleman, Daniel, Richard E. Boyatzis, and Annie McKee. *Primal Leadership: Realizing the Power of Emotional Intelligence.* Boston, MA: Harvard Business School Press, 2002.

Goleman and colleagues work on focusing aspects of emotional intelligence on leadership. An important work for leaders considering how their emotional strengths and weaknesses can impact running an organization.

- Jaworski, Joseph, and Betty S. Flowers. *Synchronicity: The Inner Path of Leadership.* San Francisco, CA: Berrett-Koehler Publishers, 1996.

Jaworski, a former business executive, relates the path he took to developing strong leadership skills through personal growth and understanding.

- Collins, James C., and Jerry I. Porras. *Built to Last: Successful Habits of Visionary Companies.* New York: Harper Business, 1994.

The enormous best seller on successful companies provides useful information on the leadership needed for that success.

- Collins, James C. *Good to Great: Why Some Companies Make the Leap—and Others Don't.* New York: Harper Business, 2001.

  Collins' follow-up to *Built to Last* that has more insights related to successful leadership.

- Senge, Peter M. "Transforming the Practice of Management." *Human Resource Development Quarterly* 4 (1993): 5–37.

  The renowned author of *The Fifth Discipline*, which gave us the idea of learning organizations, Senge brings the insights from that work into displaying the type of leadership needed for the modern learning organization.

- Wheatley, Margaret J. *Leadership and the New Science.* San Francisco, CA: Berrett-Koehler Publishers, 1992.

  This landmark work introduces the insights gained from research in the sciences drawn from a better understanding of the quantum world that showed the problem with the linear and predictive ideas that generally drive organizational and leadership studies. Wheatley charted a new path for thinking about leadership based on the new research derived from the hard sciences.

Notes

CHAPTER 1: "THE EMOTIONAL MAZE OF LEADERSHIP"

1. Joseph L. Badaracco, Jr., *Defining Moments: When Managers Must Choose between Right and Right* (Boston: Harvard Business School Press, 1997).

2. P. Ekman, "All Emotions Are Basic," in *The Nature of Emotion: Fundamental Questions*, ed. P. Ekman and R.J. Davidson (New York: Oxford University Press, 1994); Howard M. Weiss, "Conceptual and Empirical Foundations for the Study of Affect at Work," in *Emotions in the Workplace: Understanding the Structure and Role of Emotions in Organizational Behavior*, ed. Robert G. Lord, Richard J. Klimoski, and Ruth Kanfer (San Francisco, CA: Jossey-Bass, 2002).

3. Corey Robin, *Fear: The History of a Political Idea* (New York: Oxford University Press, 2004).

4. Edmund T. Rolls, *Emotion Explained* (Oxford: Oxford University Press, 2005), 450.

5. Richard C. Maddock and Richard L. Fulton, *Motivation, Emotions, and Leadership* (Westport: Quorum Books, 1998), 15.

6. L. Iacocca, *Iacocca: An Autobiography* (New York: Bantam Books, 1984), 230.

7. Robert G. Lord and Douglas J. Brown, *Leadership Processes and Follower Self-Identity* (Mahwah, NJ: Lawrence Erlbaum Associates Publishers, 2004).

8. C. Norris-Watts and R.G. Lord, "Women and Leadership: A Motivational Explanation of Stereotype Threat" (2002). Unpublished manuscript cited in Robert G. Lord and Douglas J. Brown, *Leadership Processes and Follower Identity* (Mahwah, NJ: Lawrence Erlbaum Associates, 2004), p. 141.

9. Sam M. Intrator, "Beginning Teachers and the Emotional Drama of the Classroom," *Journal of Teacher Education* 57(3) (2006): 235.

10. Badaracco, *Defining Moments: When Managers Must Choose between Right and Right*, 44–45.

11. Daniel Goleman, *Emotional Intelligence: Why It Can Matter More Than IQ* (New York: Bantam Books, 1995).

12. Peter Salovey and John D. Mayer, "Emotional Intelligence," *Imagination, Cognition and Personality* 9(3) (1990): 189.

13. John D. Mayer and Peter Salovey, "The Intelligence of Emotional Intelligence," *Intelligence* 17 (1993): 440.

14. Rick Ginsberg and Timothy Gray Davies, "The Emotional Side of Leadership," in *Effective Educational Leadership*, ed. Nigel Bennett, Megan Crawford, and Marion Cartwright (London: Paul Chapman Publishing, 2003).

CHAPTER 2: FRAMING THE ISSUES

1. Daniel Goleman, Richard E. Boyatzis, and Annie McKee, *Primal Leadership: Realizing the Power of Emotional Intelligence* (Boston: Harvard Business School Press, 2002), 3.

2. Rick Ginsberg, "The New Institutionalism, the New Science, Persistence and Change: The Power of Faith in Schools," in *The Politics of Education and the New Institutionalism*, ed. Robert L. Crowson, William Lowe Boyd, and Hanne B. Mawhinney (Washington, DC: Falmer Press, 1996); Gretchen B. Rossman, H. Dick Corbett, and William A. Firestone, *Change and Effectiveness in Schools: A Cultural Perspective* (Albany: State University of New York Press, 1988).

3. Murray Gell-Mann, *The Quark and the Jaguar: Adventures in the Simple and the Complex* (New York: W.H. Freeman and Company, 1994); John H. Holland, *Hidden Order: How Adaptation Builds Complexity* (Reading, MA: Helix Books, 1995); Ilya Priogogine and Isabelle Stengers, *Order Out of Chaos: Man's New Dialogue with Nature* (New York: Bantam Books, 1984); M. Michael Waldrop, *Complexity: The Emerging Science at the Edge of Order and Chaos* (New York: Touchstone, 1992).

4. Karl Raimund Popper, *Of Clouds and Clocks: An Approach to the Problem of Rationality and the Freedom of Man*, Arthur Holly Compton Memorial Lecture (St. Louis: Washington University, 1966).

5. Anthony T. Pescosolido, "Managing Emotion: A New Role for Emergent Group Leaders," in *Emotions in Organizational Behavior*, ed. Charmine E.J. Hartel, Wilfred J. Zerbe, and Neal M. Ashkanasy (Mahwah, NJ: Lawrence Erlbaum Associates, 2005), 317–318.

6. R.D. Mann, "A Review of the Relationships between Personality and Performance in Small Groups," *Psychological Bulletin* 56 (1959): 241–270; Ralph M. Stogdill, "Personal Factors Associated with Leadership: A Survey of the Literature," *Journal of Psychology* 25 (1948): 35–71.

7. Megan Crawford, "Inventive Management and Wise Leadership," in *Effective Educational Leadership*, ed. Nigel Bennett, Megan Crawford, and Marion Cartwright (London: Paul Chapman Publishing, 2003).

8. Frederick W. Taylor, *The Principles of Scientific Management*, *Bulletin of the Taylor Society* (New York: Harper and Brothers, 1934).

9. Henry Mintzberg, "The Manager's Job, Folklore and Fact," *Harvard Business Review* 68 (1990): 163–177; Henry Mintzberg, "Managing on the Edges," *International Journal of Public Sector Management* 10(3) (1997): 131; Henry Mintzberg, *The Structuring of Organizations* (Englewood Cliffs: Prentice-Hall, 1979).

10. Karen Van Der Zee and Remko Wabeke, "Is Trait-Emotional Intelligence Simply or More Than Just a Trait?" *European Journal of Personality* 18 (2004): 248.

11. Melissa Horner, "Leadership Theory Reviewed," in *Effective Educational Leadership*, ed. Nigel Bennett, Megan Crawford, and Marion Cartwright (London: Paul Chapman Publishing, 2003).

12. Wayne K. Hoy and Cecil G. Miskel, *Educational Administration: Theory, Research, and Practice* (Columbus, GA: McGraw-Hill Companies, 2005); Paula M. Short and John T. Greer, *Leadership in Empowered Schools*, 2nd ed. (Upper Saddle River, NJ: Merrill Prentice Hall, 2002).

13. L.L. Bernard, *An Introduction to Social Psychology* (New York: Holt, 1926).

14. Neal M. Ashkanasy and Barry Tse, "Transformational Leadership as Management of Emotion: A Conceptual Review," in *Emotions in the Workplace: Research, Theory, and Practice*, ed. Neal M. Ashkanasy, Charmine E.J. Hartel, and Wilfred J. Zerbe (Westport, CT: Quorum Books, 2000); M. Bagshaw and C. Bagshaw, "Leadership in the Twenty-First Century," *Industrial and Commercial Training* 31(6) (1999): 236; Goleman, Boyatzis, and McKee, *Primal Leadership: Realizing the Power of Emotional Intelligence*; S. Nelton, "Leadership for a New Age," *Nation's Business* 85(5) (1997): 18; Pescosolido, "Managing Emotion: A New Role for Emergent Group Leaders."

15. R. Kahn and D. Katz, "Leadership Practices in Relation to Productivity and Morale," in *Group Dynamics: Research and Theory*, ed. D. Cartwright and A. Zander (Elmsford, NY: Row, Paterson, 1960).

16. Robert R. Blake and Jane S. Mouton, *The Managerial Grid Iii* (Houston, TX: Gulf, 1985); Fred E. Fiedler, *A Theory of Leadership Effectiveness* (New York: McGraw-Hill, 1967); Paul Hersey, *The Situational Leader* (New York: Warner Books, 1985); Paul Hersey and Kenneth A. Blanchard, *Management of Organizational Behavior: Utilizing Human Resources* (Englewood Cliffs: Prentice-Hall, 1982); Robert J. House, "A Path-Goal Theory of Leader Effectiveness," in *Current Developments in the Study of Leadership*, ed. Edwin A. Fleishman and James G. Hunt (Carbondale: Southern Illinois University Press, 1973); Robert J. House and Terence R. Mitchell, "Path-Goal Theory of Leadership," *Journal of Contemporary Business* 10(3) (1974): 81–97; Hoy and Miskel, *Educational Administration: Theory, Research, and Practice*; Pescosolido, "Managing Emotion: A New Role for Emergent Group Leaders."

17. A. Baron, "Going Public with Studies on Cultural Management," *People Management* 1(19) (1995): 60; Lee G. Bolman and Terrence E. Deal, *Reframing Organizations: Artistry, Choice and Leadership* (San Francisco, CA: Jossey-Bass), 1991.

18. Ashkanasy and Tse, "Transformational Leadership as Management of Emotion: A Conceptual Review"; Richard C. Maddock and Richard L. Fulton, *Motivation, Emotions, and Leadership* (Westport, CT: Quorum Books, 1998); Pescosolido, "Managing Emotion: A New Role for Emergent Group Leaders."

19. E.L. Bell and S.M. Nkomo, "Re-visioning Women Managers' Lives," in *Gendering Organizational Theory*, ed. A. Mills and P. Tancred-Sheriff (Newbury Park, CA: Sage, 1992); Lee G. Bolman and Terrence E. Deal, *Leading with Soul: An Uncommon Journey of Spirit* (San Francisco, CA: Jossey-Bass, 2001); Sally Helgesen, *The Female Advantage: Women's Ways of Leadership* (New York: Doubleday Currency, 1990); Cecilia Reynolds, *Women and School Leadership* (Albany: State University of New York Press, 2002); Scott Thompson, *Leading from the Eye of the Storm: Spirituality and Public School Improvement* (Lanham, MD: Rowman and Littlefield Education, 2005).

20. C.C. Manz and H.P. Sims Jr., *Superleadership* (New York: Prentice-Hall, 1989).

21. Lars G. Bjork and D. Keith Gurley, "Superintendents as Transformative Leaders: Schools as Learning Communities and Communities of Learners," *Journal of Thought* 38(4) (2003): 37–78.

22. Margaret J. Wheatley, *Leadership and the New Science* (San Francisco, CA: Berrett-Koehler Publishers, 1992).

23. Peter M. Senge, "Transforming the Practice of Management," *Human Resource Development Quarterly* 4(1) (1993): 5–32.

24. Bernard M. Bass, *The Bass and Stodgill Handbook of Leadership: Theory, Research, and Managerial Applications*, 3rd ed. (New York: Free Press, 1990); Bernard M. Bass, "From Transactional to Transformational Leadership: Learning to Share the Vision," *Organizational Dynamics* 18(3) (1990): 19–32; Bernard M. Bass and Bruce J. Avolio, "The Implications of Transactional and Transformational Leadership for Individual, Team, and Organizational Development," *Research in Organizational Change and Development* 4 (1990): 231–272.

25. Joesph C. Rost, *Leadership for the Twenty First-Century* (New York: Praeger, 1991).

26. Robert J. House, "A 1976 Theory of Charismatic Leadership," in *Leadership: The Cutting Edge*, ed. J.G. Hunt and L.L. Larson (Carbondale: Southern Illinois University Press, 1977).

27. Jack Harris and B. Kim Barnes, "Inspirational Leadership: Involving Senior Leaders in Developing the Next Generation," *Industrial and Commercial Training* 38(4) (2006): 196–200.

28. Bass and Avolio, "The Implications of Transactional and Transformational Leadership for Individual, Team, and Organizational Development."

29. Ashkanasy and Tse, "Transformational Leadership as Management of Emotion: A Conceptual Review."

30. James MacGregor Burns, *Transforming Leadership: A New Pursuit of Happiness* (New York: Atlantic Monthly Press, 2003), 231.

31. Goleman, Boyatzis, and McKee, *Primal Leadership: Realizing the Power of Emotional Intelligence*, 5.

32. Ibid., 18.

33. Pescosolido, "Managing Emotion: A New Role for Emergent Group Leaders."

34. K. Grint, "The Arts of Leadership," in *Effective Educational Leadership*, ed. Nigel Bennett, Megan Crawford, and Marion Cartwright (London: Paul Chapman Publishing, 2003).

35. Neal M. Ashkanasy, "Organizational Culture: Emotion or Cognitions?" *Managerial and Organizational Cognition Interest Group Newsletter* 5(2) (1995): 1.

36. Dorthe Eide, "Emotions: From 'Ugly Duckling' Via 'Invisible Asset' Toward an Ontological Reframing," in *Emotions in Organizational Behavior*, ed. Neal M. Ashkanasy, Charmine E.J. Hartel and Wilfred J. Zerbe (Mahwah, NJ: Lawrence Erlbaum Associates, 2005), 15.

37. Charles R. Darwin, *The Expression of Emotions in Man and Animals* (Chicago: University of Chicago Press, 1995).

38. William James, "What Is Emotion?" *Mind* 9 (1884): 188–205.

39. Neal M. Ashkanasy, Charmine E.J. Hartel, and Wilfred J. Zerbe, "Emotions in the Workplace: Research, Theory, and Practice," in *Emotions in the Workplace: Research, Theory, and Practice*, ed. Neal M. Ashkanasy, Charmine E.J. Hartel, and Wilfred J. Zerbe (Westport, CT: Quorum Books, 2000), 4.

40. P.R. Kleinginna and A.M. Kleinginna, "A Categorized List of Emotion Definitions, with Suggestions for a Consensual Definition," *Motivation and Emotion* 5 (1981).

41. Ashkanasy, Hartel, and Zerbe, "Emotions in the Workplace: Research, Theory, and Practice," 11. See also K.T. Strongman, *The Psychology of Emotion: Theories of Emotion in Perspective*, 4th ed. (Chichester, UK: Wiley, 1996).

42. Edmund T. Rolls, *Emotion Explained* (Oxford: Oxford University Press, 2005), 11.

43. Peter Salovey and John D. Mayer, "Emotional Intelligence," *Imagination, Cognition and Personality* 9(3) (1990): 186.

44. Robert G. Lord and Jennifer L. Harvey, "An Information Processing Framework for Emotional Regulation," in *Emotions in the Workplace: Understanding the Structure and Role of Emotions in Organizational Behavior*, ed. Richard J. Klimoski, Ruth Kanfer, and Robert G. Lord (San Francisco, CA: Jossey-Bass, 2002).

45. C.E. Izzard, "Four Systems for Emotion Activation: Cognitive and Noncognitive Processes," *Psychological Review* 100 (1993): 68–90.

46. 1 Arne Naess, *Livsfilosofi. Et Personlig Bidrag Om Folelser Og Fornuft* (Oslo: Universitetsforlaget, 1998), 24. Quoted in Eide, "Emotions: From 'Ugly Duckling' Via 'Invisible Asset' Toward an Ontological Reframing."

47. P. Ekman, "Facial Expression and Emotion," *American Psychologist* 48 (1993): 384–392; Gerald Matthews, Moshe Zeidner, and Richard D. Roberts, *Emotional Intelligence: Science and Myth* (Cambridge, MA: A Bradford Book, MIT Press, 2002); Robert Plutchik, "A General Psychoevolutionary Theory of Emotion," in *Emotion: Theory, Research, and Experience*, ed. R. Plutchik and H. Kellerman (San Diego, CA: Academic Press, 1980); Robert Plutchik, *The Psychology and Biology of Emotion* (New York: Harper-Collins, 1994).

48. David R. Caruso and Peter Salovey, *The Emotionally Intelligent Manager: How to Develop and Use the Four Key Emotional Skills of Leadership* (San Francisco, CA: Jossey-Bass, 2004).

49. Antonio R. Damasio, *Descartes' Error: Emotion, Reason, and the Human Brain* (New York: Avon Books, 1994).

50. Michael Lewis, "The Emergence of Human Emotions," in *Handbook of Emotions*, ed. Michael Lewis and Jeannette M. Haviland (New York: Guilford Press, 1993). See also Matthew P. Spackman, "Infants and Emotions: How the Ancients' Theories Inform Modern Issues," *Cognition and Emotion* 13(6) (1999): 795–811.

51. Izzard, "Four Systems for Emotion Activation: Cognitive and Noncognitive Processes." See also Caruso and Salovey, *The Emotionally Intelligent Manager: How to Develop and Use the Four Key Emotional Skills of Leadership*; Matthews, *Emotional Intelligence: Science and Myth*.

52. Arlee R. Hochschild, *The Managed Heart: Commercialization of Human Feeling* (Berkeley: University of California Press, 1983). See also B.E. Ashforth and R.H. Humphrey, "Emotional Labor in Service Roles: The Influence of Identity," *Academy of Management Review* 18(1) (1993): 88–116; J.A. Morris and D.C. Feldman, "The Dimensions, Antecedents, and Consequences of Emotional Labor," *Academy of Management Review* 21(4) (1996): 986–1011.

53. Erving Goffman, *The Presentation of Self in Everyday Life* (New York: Doubleday Anchor, 1959).

54. L.L. Putnam and D.K. Mumby, "Organizations, Emotion and the Myth of Rationality," in *Emotion in Organizations*, ed. S. Fineman (Newbury Park, CA: Sage, 1993); Robert S. Rubin, Vicki M. Staebler Tardino, Catherine S. Daus, and David Munz, "A Reconceptualization of the Emotional Labor Construct: On the Development of an Integrated Theory of Perceived Emotional Dissonance and Emotional Labor," in *Emotions in Organizational Behavior*, ed. Charmine E.J. Hartel, Wilfred J. Zerbe, and Neal M. Ashkanasy (Mahwah, NJ: Lawrence Erlbaum Associates, 2005).

55. Rubin, Tardino, Daus, and Munz, "A Reconceptualization of the Emotional Labor Construct: On the Development of an Integrated Theory of Perceived Emotional Dissonance and Emotional Labor."

56. Walter B. Cannon, *The Wisdom of the Body* (New York: Norton, 1931).

57. Hans Selye, *The Stress of Life* (New York: McGraw-Hill, 1956).

58. S. Cartwright and C.L. Cooper, "Coping in Occupational Settings," in *Handbook of Coping*, ed. M. Zeidner and N.S. Endler (New York: Wiley, 1996).

59. C. Maslach and S.E. Jackson, *The Maslach Burnout Inventory* (Palo Alto, CA: Consulting Psychologist Press, 1981); C. Maslach and S.E. Jackson, "The Measurement of Experienced Burnout," *Journal of Occupational Behavior* 2 (1981): 99–113; C. Maslach and S.E. Jackson, "Patterns of Burnout among a National Sample of Public Contact Workers," *Journal of Health and Human Resources Administration* 7 (1984): 189–212.

60. A.J. Elkin and P.J. Rosch, "Promoting Mental Health at the Workplace: The Prevention Side of Stress Management," *Occupational Medicine: State of the Art Review* 5 (1990): 739–754; Robert Karasek and Tores Theorell, *Healthy Work: Stress Productivity and the Reconstruction of Working Life* (New York: Wiley, 1990).

61. R. Pekrun and M. Frese, "Emotions in Work and Achievement," in *International Review of Industrial and Organizational Psychology*, ed. C.I. Cooper and I.T. Robertson (Chichester, UK: Wiley, 1992).

62. Mark Slaski and Susan Cartwright, "Emotional Intelligence Training and Its Implications for Stress, Health and Performance," *Stress and Health* 19 (2003): 234.

63. Caruso and Salovey, *The Emotionally Intelligent Manager: How to Develop and Use the Four Key Emotional Skills of Leadership*, 52.

64. S. Douglas Pugh, "Emotional Regulation in Individuals and Dyads," in *Emotions in the Workplace: Understanding the Structure and Role of Emotions in Organizational Behavior*, ed. Richard J. Klimoski, Ruth Kanfer, and Robert G. Lord (San Francisco, CA: Jossey-Bass, 2002), 161.

65. R.G. Lord, D.J. Brown, and S.J. Freiberg, "Understanding the Dynamics of Leadership: The Role of Follower Self-Concepts in the Leader/Follower Relationship," *Organizational Behavior and Human Decision Processes* 78 (1999): 171.

66. Elaine Hatfield, John T. Cacioppo, and Richard L. Rapson, *Emotional Contagion* (Cambridge: Cambridge University Press, 1994). See also Paul D. Cherulnik, Kristina A. Donley, Tay-Sha R. Wiewel, Susan R. Miller, "Charisma Is Contagious: The Effect of Leader's Charisma on Observers' Affect," *Journal of Applied Social Psychology* 31 (2001): 2149–2159.

67. J.J. Gross and O.P. John, "Revealing Feelings: Facets of Emotional Expressivity in Self-Reports, Peer Ratings, and Behavior," *Journal of Personality and Social Psychology* 72 (1997): 435–448; Pugh, "Emotional Regulation in Individuals and Dyads."

68. Goleman, Boyatzis, and McKee, *Primal Leadership: Realizing the Power of Emotional Intelligence*, 8.

69. David Wechlser, *The Measurement and Appraisal of Adult Intelligence* (Baltimore, MD: Williams & Wilkins, 1958).

70. E.L. Thorndike, "Intelligence and Its Uses," *Harper's Magazine* 140 (1920): 227–235.

71. R.L. Thorndike and S. Stein, "An Evaluation of the Attempts to Measure Social Intelligence," *Psychological Bulletin* 34 (1937): 275–284.

72. Lee J. Cronbach, *Essentials of Psychological Testing*, 2nd ed. (New York: Harper and Row, 1960).

73. Nancy Cantor and John F. Kihlstrom, *Personality and Social Intelligence* (Englewood Cliffs, NJ: Prentice Hall, 1987); John F. Kihlstrom and Nancy Cantor, "Social Intelligence," in *Handbook of Intelligence*, ed. Robert J. Sternberg (New York: Cambridge University Press, 2000); R.J. Sternberg and C.A. Smith, "Social Intelligence and Decoding Skills in Nonverbal Communication," *Social Cognition* 3 (1985): 168–192.

74. Robert J. Sternberg, *Successful Intelligence: How Practical and Creative Intelligence Determine Success in Life* (New York: Plume, 1996). See also work on "pragmatic intelligence," Robert. J. Sternberg and David R. Caruso, "Practical Modes of Knowing," in *Learning and Teaching the Ways of Knowing: 84th Yearbook of the*

National Society for the Study of Education (Part II), ed. Elliot Eisner (Chicago: University of Chicago Press, 1985).

75. Howard Gardner, *Frames of Mind: The Theory of Multiple Intelligences* (New York: Basic Books, 1983); Howard Gardner, *Multiple Intelligences: The Theory in Practice* (New York: Basic Books, 1993).

76. Gardner, *Multiple Intelligences: The Theory in Practice*, 23.

77. Ibid., 25.

78. Daniel Goleman, *Social Intelligence: The New Science of Social Relationships* (New York: Bantam Books, 2006).

79. John D. and Peter Salovey Mayer, "What Is Emotional Intelligence?" in *Emotional Development and Emotional Intelligence: Educational Implications*, ed. Peter Salovey and David J. Sluyter (New York: Basic Books, 1997), 10.

80. Reuven Bar-On, "Emotional and Social Intelligence," in *The Handbook of Emotional Intelligence*, ed. R. Bar-On and J.D.A. Parker (San Francisco, CA: Jossey-Bass, 2000); Victor Dulewicz and Malcolm Higgs, "Can Emotional Intelligence Be Measured and Developed?" *Leadership and Organization Development Journal* 20(5) (1999): 242–252; Matthews, *Emotional Intelligence: Science and Myth*; Benjamin R. Palmer, Gilles Gignac, Ramesh Manocha, and Con Stough, "A Psychometric Evaluation of the Mayer-Salovey-Caruso Emotional Intelligence Test Version 2.0," *Intelligence* 33 (2005): 285–305; David L. Van Rooy and Chockalingam Viswesvaran, "Emotional Intelligence: A Meta-Analytic Investigation of Predictive Validity and Nomological Net," *Journal of Vocational Behavior* 65 (2004): 71–95.

81. Victor Dulewicz and Malcolm Higgs, "Emotional Intelligence: A Review and Evaluation Study," *Journal of Managerial Psychology* 15(4) (2000): 341–372; Rooy and Viswesvaran, "Emotional Intelligence: A Meta-Analytic Investigation of Predictive Validity and Nomological Net."

82. H.W. Goldstein, S. Zedeck, and I.L. Goldstein, "G: Is This Your Final Answer?" *Human Performance* 15 (2002): 123; J.E. Hunter and R.F. Hunter, "Validity and Utility of Alternative Predictors of Job Performance," *Psychological Bulletin* 96(1) (1984): 72–98.

83. Daniel Goleman, *Emotional Intelligence: Why It Can Matter More Than IQ* (New York: Bantam Books, 1995), 28.

84. Daniel Goleman, *Working with Emotional Intelligence* (New York: Bantam Books, 1998).

85. Neal M. Ashkanasy and Catherine Daus, "Rumors of the Death of Emotional Intelligence in Organizational Behavior Are Vastly Exaggerated," *Journal of Organizational Behavior* 26 (2005): 441–453.

86. Cliona Diggens, "Emotional Intelligence: The Key to Effective Performance," *Human Resource Management* 12(1) (2004): 33–35.

87. Matthews, *Emotional Intelligence: Science and Myth*.

88. Goleman, *Emotional Intelligence: Why It Can Matter More Than IQ*, 285.

89. Matthews, *Emotional Intelligence: Science and Myth*, 513.

90. John D. Mayer and Casey D. Cobb, "Educational Policy on Emotional Intelligence: Does It Make Sense?" *Educational Psychology Review* 12(2) (2000): 176.

91. Robert K. Cooper and Ayman Sawaf, *Executive EQ: Emotional Intelligence in Leadership & Organizations* (New York: Grosset/Putnam, 1996).

92. Daniel Goleman, "What Makes a Leader?" *Harvard Business Review* 76(6) (1999): 94.

93. Steven R. Covey, *The Seven Habits of Highly Successful People: Restoring the Character Ethic* (New York: Simon and Schuster, 1990).

94. Henry B. Reiff, Paul J. Gerber, and Rick Ginsberg, *Exceeding Expectations: Successful Adults with Learning Disabilities* (Austin, TX: Pro-Ed, 1997), 89.

95. J.G. Leslie and E. Van Velsor, *A Look at Derailment Today: North America and Europe* (Greensboro: Center for Creative Leadership, 1996); M.W. McCall and M.M. Lombardo, *Off the Track: Why and How Successful Executives Get Derailed* (Greensboro, NC: Center for Creative Leadership, 1983).

96. S.V. Dulewicz and P.J.A. Herbert, "Predicting Advancement to Senior Management from Competencies and Personality Data: A 7-Year Follow-up Study," *British Journal of Management* 10(1) (1999): 13–22.

97. Thomas J. Peters and Nancy Austin, *A Passion for Excellence: The Leadership Difference* (New York: Random House, 1985).

98. Thomas J. Peters, "Leadership and Emotion" (Palo Alto, CA: TPG Communications, 1989).

99. Chris Argyris, "Double Loop Learning in Organizations," *Harvard Business Review* 55(5) (1977): 115–126.

100. Chester I. Barnard, *The Functions of the Executive* (Cambridge, MA: Harvard University Press, 1938).

101. Ibid.

102. Robert L. Katz, "Skills of an Effective Administrator," *Harvard Business Review* 34 (1955): 34.

103. Garth Morgan, *Images of Organizations* (Thousand Oaks, CA: Sage, 1998), 192.

104. Stephen Fineman, ed., *Emotion in Organization* (Newbury Park, CA: Sage, 1993), 25.

105. Ibid., 9–10.

106. I.L. Mangham, "Emotional Discourse in Organizations," in *Discourse and Organization*, ed. David Grant, Tom Keenoy, and Cliff Oswick (Thousand Oaks, CA: Sage, 1998), 51.

CHAPTER 3: THE EYE OF THE STORM

1. Michael Hammer and James Champy, *Reengineering the Corporation: A Manifesto for Business Revolution* (New York: HarperBusiness, 1993).

2. Kent D. Peterson, "The Principal's Tasks," *Administrator's Notebook* 26(8) (1977–1978): 1–4.

3. Rick Ginsberg and Timothy Gray Davies, "The Emotional Side of Leadership," in *Effective Educational Leadership*, ed. Nigel Bennett, Megan Crawford, and Marion Cartwright (London: Paul Chapman Publishing, 2003).

4. Michael Scriven has labeled the common dislike of being evaluated as valuephobia. Likely, there is an equally common dislike for conducting evaluations. See Michael Scriven, "Evaluation Ideologies," in *Evaluation Models: Viewpoints on Educational and Human Services Evaluation*, ed. George F. Madaus, Michael Scriven, and Daniel L. Sufflebeam (Boston: Kluwer-Nijhoff, 1987).

5. C. Maslach and S.E. Jackson, "The Measurement of Experienced Burnout," *Journal of Occupational Behavior* 2 (1981): 99–113; C. Maslach and S.E. Jackson, "Patterns of Burnout among a National Sample of Public Contact Workers," *Journal of Health and Human Resources Administration* 7 (1984): 189–212.

6. Albert O. Hirschman, *Exit, Voice, and Loyalty: Responses to Declines in Firms, Organizations, and States* (Cambridge, MA: Harvard University Press, 1970).

7. A.M. Bloch, "Combat Neurosis in Inner-City Schools," *American Journal of Psychiatry* 10 (1978): 1189–1192.

8. Arlee R. Hochschild, *The Managed Heart: Commercialization of Human Feeling* (Berkeley: University of California Press, 1983).

9. Alicia A. Grandey and Analea L. Brauburger, "The Emotion Regulation Behind the Customer Service Smile," in *Emotions in the Workplace: Understanding the Structure and Role of Emotions in Organizational Behavior*, ed. Richard J. Klimoski, Ruth Kanfer, and Robert G. Lord (San Francisco, CA: Jossey-Bass, 2002); Hochschild, *The Managed Heart: Commercialization of Human Feeling*; Robert S. Rubin, Vicki M. Staebler Tardino, Catherine S. Daus, and David Munz, "A Reconceptualization of the Emotion Labor Construct: On the Development of an Integrated Theory of Perceived Emotional Dissonance and Emotional Labor," in *Emotions in Organizational Behavior*, ed. Charmine E.J. Hartel, Wilfred J. Zerbe, and Neal M. Ashkanasy (Mahwah, NJ: Lawrence Erlbaum Associates, 2005).

10. A.A. Grandey, "Emotion Regulation in the Workplace: A New Way to Conceptualize Emotional Labor," *Journal of Occupational Health Psychology* 5(1) (2000): 95–110.

11. Ibid.; Hochschild, *The Managed Heart: Commercialization of Human Feeling*; Rubin, Tardino, Daus, and Munz, "A Reconceptualization of the Emotion Labor Construct: On the Development of an Integrated Theory of Perceived Emotional Dissonance and Emotional Labor."

CHAPTER 4: EXTRA GRACE REQUIRED

1. Reverend Andrew D. Burns, *Extra Grace Required!* (Emmanuel Tabernacle, 2006 [cited January 18, 2006]); available from http://www.lifeapp.org/pdf/Extra%20Grace%20Required.pdf.

2. David J. O'Leary, "When You Feel Like Giving Up on Someone," *At The Center Magazine* (1) (2004): 1, http://www.atcmag.com/v5n1/article5.asp.

3. Robert I. Sutton, *The No Asshole Rule: Building a Civilized Workplace and Surviving One That Isn't* (New York: Warner Business Books 2007).

4. Barbara Woodhouse, *No Bad Dogs: The Woodhouse Way* (New York: Simon and Schuster, 1984), 70.

5. *Monitor on Psychology* 37(7) (2006).

6. Lauri Meyers, "Still Wearing the 'Kick Me' Sign," *Monitor on Psychology* 37(7) (2006): 70.

7. Ibid., 69.

CHAPTER 5: COPING WITH EMOTIONS ON THE JOB

1. Gary Hamel and C.K. Prahalad, "Corporate Imagination and Expeditionary Marketing," *Harvard Business Review* 69(4) (1991): 81.

2. http://www.mytherapybuddy.com.

3. See, for example, Beverly Potter, *Beating Job Burnout: How to Transform Work Pressure into Productivity* (Berkeley: Ronin, 1985).

4. Zak Stambor, "Bullying Stems from Fear, Apathy," *Monitor on Psychology* 37(1) (2006).

5. C.R. Snyder and Shane J. Lopez, eds., *Handbook of Positive Psychology* (New York: Oxford University Press, 2002).

6. Rick Ginsberg, "The New Institutionalism, the New Science, Persistence and Change: The Power of Faith in Schools," in *The Politics of Education and the New Institutionalism*, ed. Robert L. Crowson, William Lowe Boyd, and Hanne B. Mawhinney (Washington, DC: Falmer Press, 1996); John H. Holland, *Hidden Order: How Adaptation Builds Complexity* (Reading, MA: Helix Books, 1995); Ilya Priogogine and Isabelle Stengers, *Order Out of Chaos: Man's New Dialogue with Nature* (New York: Bantam Books, 1984); M. Michael Waldrop, *Complexity: The Emerging Science at the Edge of Order and Chaos* (New York: Touchstone, 1992).

7. Franz Capra, *The Turning Point* (New York: Bantam Books, 1982), 47.

8. Priogogine and Stengers, *Order Out of Chaos: Man's New Dialogue with Nature*.

9. Margaret J. Wheatley, *Leadership and the New Science* (San Francisco, CA: Berrett-Koehler Publishers, 1992), 7.

10. Kenneth W. Thomas and Ralph H. Kilmann, *Thomas-Killman Conflict Mode Instrument* (Palo Alto, CA: Xicom: Consulting Psychologist Press, 1974).

CHAPTER 6: PLANNING FOR AN EMOTIONAL FUTURE

1. David R. Caruso and Peter Salovey, *The Emotionally Intelligent Manager: How to Develop and Use the Four Key Emotional Skills of Leadership* (San Francisco, CA: Jossey-Bass, 2004), 24.

2. H. Hopfl and S. Linstead, "Learning to Feel and Feeling to Learn: Emotion and Learning in Organisations," *Management Learning* 28(1) (1997): 5.

3. Henry B. Reiff, Paul J. Gerber, and Rick Ginsberg, *Exceeding Expectations: Successful Adults with Learning Disabilities* (Austin: Pro-Ed, 1997), 101.

4. Available from http://www.cert.org/octave/.

5. Dorthe Eide, "Emotions: From 'Ugly Duckling' Via 'Invisible Asset' Toward an Ontological Reframing," in "Emotions in Organizational Behavior," ed. Neal M. Ashkanasy, Charmine E.J. Hartel and Wilfred J. Zerbe (Mahwah, NJ: Lawrence Erlbaum Associates, 2005).

6. J.J. Gross, "The Emerging Field of Emotional Regulation: An Integrated Review," *Review of General Psychology* 2(3) (1998): 275.

7. Gerald Matthews, Moshe Zeidner, and Richard D. Roberts, *Emotional Intelligence: Science and Myth* (Cambridge, MA: A Bradford Book, MIT Press, 2002), 472.

8. Gross, "The Emerging Field of Emotional Regulation: An Integrated Review." See also Robert G. Lord and Jennifer L. Harvey, "An Information Processing Framework for Emotional Regulation," in *Emotions in the Workplace: Understanding the Structure and Role of Emotions in Organizational Behavior*, ed. Robert G. Lord, Richard J. Klimoski, and Ruth Kanfer (San Francisco, CA: Jossey-Bass, 2002).

9. Gross, "The Emerging Field of Emotional Regulation: An Integrated Review," 287.

10. Matthews, Zeidner, and Roberts, *Emotional Intelligence: Science and Myth*, 505.

11. Maureen Buckley and Carolyn Saarni, "Skills of Emotional Competence: Developmental Implications," in *Emotional Intelligence in Everyday Life*, ed. James Ciarrochi, Joseph P. Forgas, and John D. Mayer (New York: Psychology Press, 2006), 55.

12. Dan Goleman, "An EI-Based Theory of Performance," in *The Emotionally Intelligent Workplace: How to Select for, Measure and Improve EI in Individuals, Groups and Organizations*, ed. Cary Cherniss and Dan Goleman (San Francisco, CA: Jossey-Bass, 2001).

13. Carolyn Saarni, "Emotional Competence: A Developmental Perspective," in *Handbook on Emotional Intelligence: Theory, Development, Assessment and Application at Home, School, and in the Workplace*, ed. R. Bar-On and J.D.A. Parker (San Francisco, CA: Jossey-Bass, 2000).

14. R.D. Lane, D.M. Quinlan, G.E. Schwartz, P.A. Walker, and S.B. Zeitlin, "The Levels of Emotional Awareness Scale: A Cognitive-Development Measure of Emotion," *Journal of Personality Assessment* 55 (1990): 124–134; R.D. Lane and G.E. Schwartz, "Levels of Emotional Awareness: A Cognitive-Developmental Theory and Its Application to Psychopathology," *American Journal of Psychiatry* 144 (1987): 133–143.

15. Matthews, Zeidner, and Roberts, *Emotional Intelligence: Science and Myth*, 471.

16. Joan M. Vitello-Cicciu, "Innovative Leadership through Emotional Intelligence," *Nursing Management* 34(10) (2003): 31.

17. Caruso and Salovey, *The Emotionally Intelligent Manager: How to Develop and Use the Four Key Emotional Skills of Leadership*, 9. See also David R. Caruso, Brian Bienn, and Susan A. Kornacki, "Emotional Intelligence in the Workplace," in *Emotional Intelligence in Everyday Life*, ed. Joseph Ciarrochi, Joseph P. Forgas, and John D. Mayer (New York: Psychology Press, 2006).

18. Caruso and Salovey, *The Emotionally Intelligent Manager: How to Develop and Use the Four Key Emotional Skills of Leadership*, 30.

19. Kate G. Niederhoffer and James W. Pennebaker, "Sharing One's Story: On the Benefits of Writing or Talking About Emotional Experience," in *Handbook of Positive Psychology*, ed. C.R. Snyder and Shane J. Lopez (New York: Oxford University Press, 2002).

CHAPTER 7: EPILOGUE

1. Barry Glassner, *The Culture of Fear: Why Americans Are Afraid of the Wrong Things* (New York: Basic Books, 1999).
2. J. Krishnamurti, *On Fear* (San Francisco, CA: HarperCollins, 1995).

Index

About the Authors

RICK GINSBERG is Dean of the School of Education at the University of Kansas. Previously, he served as Professor and Director of the School of Education at Colorado State University. He has spent nearly thirty years in education, in teaching, research, administration, and policy. He is the author of over eighty journal articles and book chapters on issues related to individual and organizational success. He is also coeditor of two books and coauthor of *Exceeding Expectations*.

TIMOTHY GRAY DAVIES is Professor and Director of the School of Education at Colorado State University, where he previously served as Director of Graduate Programs and Program Chair of the Community College Leadership Doctoral Program. Prior to joining Colorado State, he spent over thirty years in community college development, administration, and leadership. He has published over forty articles and book chapters on leadership and emotional intelligence.